baking for baby

baking for baby

Cute cakes & cookies for baby showers,
naming days & early birthdays

Annie Rigg

photography by
Kate Whitaker

LONDON · NEW YORK

Senior Designer Iona Hoyle

Commissioning Editor
Céline Hughes

Head of Production
Patricia Harrington

Art Director Leslie Harrington

Editorial Director Julia Charles

Prop Stylist Jo Harris

Indexer Hilary Bird

First published in 2013
by Ryland Peters & Small
20–21 Jockey's Fields
London WC1R 4BW
and
519 Broadway, 5th Floor
New York, NY 10012

www.rylandpeters.com

Text © Annie Rigg 2013

Design and photographs
© Ryland Peters & Small 2013

Printed in China

10 9 8 7 6 5 4 3 2 1

ISBN: 978-1-84975-345-6

A CIP record for this book is available
from the British Library.

A CIP record for this book is available
from the Library of Congress.

notes

ⓥ All spoon measurements are level,
unless otherwise specified.

ⓥ Ovens should be preheated to the
specified temperature. Recipes in this
book were tested using a regular oven.
If using a fan-assisted/convection
oven, follow the manufacturer's
instructions for adjusting temperatures.

ⓥ All eggs are medium, unless
otherwise specified. Recipes containing
raw or partially cooked egg should not
be served to the very young, very old,
anyone with a compromised immune
system or pregnant women.

ⓥ All butter is unsalted, unless
otherwise specified.

ⓥ When a recipe calls for the grated
zest of a citrus fruit, buy unwaxed
fruit and wash well before using.
If you can only find treated fruit,
scrub well in warm soapy water
and rinse before using.

contents

6   introduction

8   basic recipes

14   baby showers

52   naming days & christenings

78   baby birthdays

124   stockists & suppliers

126   index

128   acknowledgments

introduction

Of all the parties and all the celebrations, the birth of a new baby is, for most people, at the very top of the list as the most special. Whether it's the birth of your own child, a grandchild, nephew, niece or a friend's newborn, a celebration is most certainly in order. Whatever the occasion, whether it be a baby shower, christening, naming day or the birthday of a toddler, there is no doubt going to be a need for some delicious sweet baked goods at some point.

Here is a selection of recipes that are perfect for just such joyous moments – whether you want to bake a large, occasion cake that will feed a crowd of friends and family, or a few dainty little delights to please a gathering of girls, or maybe even a tray of highly decorated cupcakes for a toddler's birthday party, there's something here for all of those celebrations and more besides.

I'm a firm believer in getting kids involved in the kitchen, even if that means simply 'helping' to ice cookies, roll and shape cake pops and, more importantly, scatter sprinkles liberally around the kitchen (and hopefully on cakes and cookies). In my experience, most children jump at the opportunity to create something that is fun to make and eat.

Baby showers are more often than not organized and attended by the close friends and family of a mum-to-be and most of the guests are likely to be women. Often the colour theme is pink or blue depending on the sex of the baby, but the underlying theme should be one of cuteness and the food that is served should reflect that. Think small, delicate, pretty, and of course, delicious. Baby showers are often afternoon-tea affairs with guests bringing along a gift for either the mum-to-be or baby and a tray of goodies to add to the tea table. Some of the bakes in the Baby Showers chapter would work beautifully as a foodie gift package. A fancy box of iced Gingerbread Babies (page 43), Marshmallows (page 36) or

Rainbow Cookies (page 44), wrapped in pretty tissue paper and tied with colourful ribbons would be sure to please and delight.

Naming days or christening teas tend to be more adult occasions and so you can design your tea menu with this in mind. I have included a simple fruitcake covered in marzipan and fondant icing (page 57). Traditionally this would have been the top tier of the child's parents' wedding cake that was kept and set aside for the christening of the first-born child. Here it's a rich fruitcake iced with a simple daisy-chain detail, but you could always pipe the name of the child on top of the cake. If you prefer your cakes to be on the smaller scale, try baking the Citrus Coconut Drizzle Cakes (page 58) or Mini Victoria Sandwiches (page 74) – both even more delectable and contemporary for being in miniature.

Children's birthday parties give you a wonderful opportunity to let your imagination go wild and to embrace your inner child. I love making edible toppers for cupcakes – I've used this idea in the Sailboat Cupcakes (page 120) but you could really run with this and create no end of double delights. My Gingerbread Birdhouse (page 102) is a twist on a festive gingerbread house but given a fun and modern edge. If you prefer your birthday bakes to be on the simpler side, there is a Banana Cake (page 115) and the all-time classic of kids' parties, Butterfly Cakes (page 90). Neither of these requires any special icing and piping skills, just some good-quality ingredients and a little quiet kitchen time.

Remember, when baking for any of these occasions, everything should be fun, look just a little fantastic and taste divine. Don't forget the sprinkles!

basic cakes

These are the basic cupcake recipes used in many of the recipes in this book. Feel free to use these as the base for your own designs, or flick through the book and see which cute cupcake creation takes your fancy.

vanilla cupcakes

This is the simplest and easiest cake mixture to make. Here I've flavoured it with pure vanilla extract but you could just as easily use lemon or orange extract, rosewater or coffee essence if you prefer.

makes 12

175 g/1½ sticks butter, soft
175 plus 2 tablespoons ¾ cup (caster) sugar
3 eggs, beaten
1 teaspoon pure vanilla extract
175 g/1⅓ cups plain/all-purpose flour
2 teaspoons baking powder
½ teaspoon bicarbonate of/baking soda
a pinch of salt
3 tablespoons sour cream, at room temperature

12-hole muffin pan, lined with paper cases

Preheat the oven to 180°C (350°F) Gas 4.

Cream the butter and sugar until pale, light and fluffy – about 3 minutes in a stand mixer. Gradually add the beaten eggs, mixing well and scraping down the side of the bowl between each addition. Add the vanilla and mix again.

Sift the flour, baking powder, bicarbonate of/baking soda and salt into the bowl, add the sour cream and fold in using a rubber spatula or a large metal spoon. Once the mixture is smooth, divide it evenly between the paper cases and bake on the middle shelf of the preheated oven for about 20 minutes or until the cakes are golden, well risen and a skewer inserted into the middle of the cakes comes out clean.

Allow the cupcakes to rest in the pan for 3–4 minutes, then transfer to a wire rack and allow to cool completely.

chocolate cupcakes

Here is a delicious and just-as-easy chocolate cupcake recipe.

makes 12–14

40 g/⅓ cup unsweetened cocoa powder
100 ml/⅓ cup plus 1 tablespoon boiling water
150 g/10 tablespoons butter, soft and cubed
175 g/generous ¾ cup (caster) sugar
2 large eggs, beaten
1 teaspoon pure vanilla extract
150 g/1 cup plus 2 tablespoons plain/all-purpose flour
2 teaspoons baking powder
½ teaspoon bicarbonate of/baking soda
a pinch of salt
2 tablespoons sour cream, at room temperature

12-hole muffin pan, lined with paper cases

Preheat the oven to 180°C (350°F) Gas 4.

Tip the cocoa into a small, heatproof bowl, add the boiling water and whisk until smooth. Set aside to cool.

Cream the butter and sugar until pale, light and fluffy – about 3 minutes in a stand mixer. Gradually add the beaten eggs, mixing well and scraping down the side of the bowl between each addition. Add the vanilla and cocoa mixture and mix again.

Sift the flour, baking powder, bicarbonate of/baking soda and salt into the bowl, add the sour cream and fold in using a rubber spatula or a large metal spoon. Once the mixture is smooth, divide it evenly between the paper cases and bake on the middle shelf of the preheated oven for about 20 minutes or until the cakes are well risen and a skewer inserted into the middle of the cakes comes out clean.

Allow the cupcakes to rest in the pan for 3–4 minutes, then transfer to a wire rack and allow to cool completely.

basic cookie doughs

gingerbread

makes about 12 large cookies

2 tablespoons golden syrup or light corn syrup
1 large egg yolk
200 g/1⅔ cups plain/all-purpose flour
½ teaspoon baking powder
1½ teaspoons ground ginger
1 teaspoon ground cinnamon
¼ teaspoon freshly grated nutmeg
a pinch of salt
100 g/7 tablespoons butter, chilled and diced
75 g/⅓ cup light muscovado or light brown
(soft) sugar

baking sheets, lined with parchment paper

Beat together the syrup and egg yolk in a small bowl.
Sift the flour, baking powder, spices and salt into a food
processor (or mixing bowl) and add the butter. Use the
pulse button to process the mixture (or rub the butter
into the flour mixture with your fingertips). When the
mixture starts to look like sand and there are no lumps
of butter, add the sugar and pulse (or mix with your
fingers) for 30 seconds to incorporate. With the motor
running, add the egg-yolk mixture and pulse (or mix
with a wooden spoon) until starting to clump together.

Tip the mixture out onto a very lightly floured surface
and knead gently to bring together into a smooth ball.
Flatten the dough into a disc, wrap in clingfilm/plastic
wrap and refrigerate for 1–2 hours.

Preheat the oven to 170°C (325°F) Gas 3.

Lightly flour the work surface and roll the dough evenly
to a thickness of 3 mm/⅛ inch. Use a cookie cutter or
template to stamp out as many cookies as possible from
the dough. Arrange the cookies on the prepared baking
sheets. Gather the dough scraps together, knead lightly,
re-roll and stamp out more cookies until all the dough
has been used up.

Bake the gingerbread in batches on the middle shelf of
the preheated oven for 10–12 minutes – you may need
to swap the sheets around to ensure that the cookies
bake evenly. Allow the cookies to cool completely on
the baking sheets before icing. Store un-iced gingerbread
cookies in an airtight box until needed.

vanilla shortbread

makes about 12 large cookies

225 g/15 tablespoons butter, soft and cubed
225 g/1 cup plus 2 tablespoons (caster) sugar
½ teaspoon pure vanilla extract
1 large egg, beaten
450 g/3½ cups plain/all-purpose flour
1 teaspoon baking powder
a pinch of salt

baking sheets, lined with parchment paper

Cream the butter and sugar with an electric whisk or
stand mixer until pale and light – about 2 minutes. Add
the grated lemon zest or extract and mix well. Add the
egg and mix until thoroughly combined.

Sift together the flour, baking powder and salt and
gradually add to the creamed mixture. Bring the
dough together into a ball using your hands.
Flatten into a fat disc, wrap in clingfilm/
plastic wrap and refrigerate until firm
or for at least 2 hours.

Preheat the oven to 170°C (325°F) Gas 3.

Lightly flour the work surface and roll the dough out evenly to a thickness of 3 mm/⅛ inch. Using cookie cutters, stamp out shapes from the dough and arrange on the prepared baking sheets. Gather the dough scraps together, press into a smooth-ish ball, re-roll and stamp out more cookies.

Bake the cookies in batches on the middle shelf of the preheated oven for about 12 minutes on the middle shelf of the preheated oven or until pale golden – you may need to swap the sheets around to ensure that the cookies brown evenly. Allow the cookies to cool on the baking sheets for about 10 minutes, then transfer to a wire rack and allow to cool completely.

To make chocolate shortbread, substitute 50 g/½ cup cocoa powder for 50 g/½ cup of the plain/all-purpose flour.

'flooding' cookies

Several recipes in this book will involve 'flooding' cookies in order to decorate them with royal icing. You will need a couple of disposable piping bags, a mini palette knife, teaspoon or small knife.

Bake your cookies and allow them to cool completely.

Take a disposable piping bag (or a piping bag with a fine writing tip) and fill it with the colour of icing you want to frame your cookie. Snip the very tip off the bag with scissors.

Carefully pipe a neat, continuous border all around each cookie. Allow to dry for 15 minutes.

Put the icing for the inside of the outline in a bowl and stir 1–2 drops of cold water into it to make it slightly runnier. Spoon some of this icing inside the border and spread it carefully up to the edges with a mini palette knife, back of a teaspoon or a small knife. This is called 'flooding'.

Allow to set before decorating and serving.

basic frostings

marshmallow frosting

250 g/1¼ cups (caster) sugar
1 tablespoon water
4 egg whites
a pinch of salt

sugar thermometer

Put all the ingredients in a heatproof bowl set over a pan of simmering water. Whisk slowly until the sugar has dissolved and the mixture is foamy. Continue cooking, whisking constantly, until the mixture has doubled in volume, looks glossy and opaque, and reaches at least 60°C (140°F) on a sugar thermometer. Immediately pour the frosting into the bowl of a stand mixer fitted with the whisk attachment (or use an electric whisk and mixing bowl) and beat on medium speed until it will stand in stiff, glossy peaks – this will take about 3 minutes. Use immediately.

chocolate ganache

200 g/6½ oz. dark/bittersweet chocolate, finely chopped (60–70% cocoa solids and no more)
225 ml/1 cup double/heavy cream
2 tablespoons light muscovado or light brown (soft) sugar
50 g/3 tablespoons butter

Put the chocolate in a medium bowl. Put the cream and sugar in a small saucepan and heat until only just boiling and the sugar has dissolved. Pour the hot cream over the chocolate and let melt for 5 minutes. Add the butter and stir gently until smooth. Let thicken to the desired consistency before using.

meringue buttercream

200 g/1 cup (caster) sugar
3 egg whites
250 g/2 sticks butter, soft and cubed
1 teaspoon pure vanilla extract

sugar thermometer

Put the sugar and egg whites in a heatproof bowl set over a pan of simmering water. Whisk slowly until the sugar has dissolved and the mixture is foamy. Continue cooking, whisking constantly, until the mixture has doubled in volume, looks glossy and opaque, and reaches at least 60°C (140°F) on a sugar thermometer. Pour into the bowl of a stand mixer fitted with the whisk attachment (or use an electric whisk and mixing bowl). Beat until the mixture has doubled in volume, cooled and will stand in stiff, glossy peaks – this will take about 3 minutes. Gradually add the butter to the cooled meringue mix, beating constantly, until the frosting is smooth. Fold in the vanilla.

To make chocolate meringue buttercream, melt 150 g/5 oz. chopped dark/bittersweet chocolate, then leave to cool slightly. Stir into the buttercream at the same time as the vanilla.

edible decorations

bootees

Tint some ready-to-roll royal icing/fondant/sugar paste your chosen colour by gradually adding food colouring paste and kneading it in until completely incorporated. Break off a piece the size of a small square of chocolate and shape it into an oval lozenge. Lay it on the work surface to flatten the bottom slightly. Take another piece the size of a hazelnut and roll into a ball. Lay this on one end of the lozenge, then push the end of a pastry brush or small wooden spoon halfway into the ball to make an indent. Smooth over the joins with your fingers. Allow to dry for at least 3 hours, and preferably overnight, before tying string around the top of each bootee.

rattles

Tint some ready-to-roll royal icing/fondant/sugar paste your chosen colour by gradually adding food colouring paste and kneading it in until completely incorporated. Break off a piece the size of a large glacé/candied cherry, roll into a ball and lay on parchment paper. Take a smaller piece and roll between your fingers into a rod roughly 2–3 cm/ 1¼ inches long. Take another, smaller piece of icing and shape into a flat, 1-cm/½-inch disc. Using a skewer, make a hole in the middle of the disc so that you now have an 'O' shape. Using a fine, clean paint brush and some food colouring paste, paint a simple line and dot pattern around the ball of the rattle. Brush a small drop of water at each end of the rod and press a ball onto one end and an 'O' onto the other. Allow to dry for at least 3 hours, and preferably overnight, before tying string around the middle of each rattle.

ladybugs

Break off a small nugget from some plain ready-to-roll royal icing/fondant/sugar-paste, wrap in clingfilm/plastic wrap and set aside to make the eyes later. Tint the remaining icing red by gradually adding red food colouring paste and kneading it in until completely incorporated. Break off a piece the size of a pecan and roll into a ball. Lay it on the work surface and flatten it slightly. Using a fine, clean paint brush and black food colouring paste, paint a triangular shape at one end of the ball for the head. Use a skewer to press an indent down the back of each ladybug from the middle of the head to the bottom of the body and paint the indent black. Paint an even number of dots on each side. Make the eyes from the reserved white icing: roll 2 tiny amounts into balls and press onto the head. Paint a small black dot in the middle of each eye. Allow to dry for at least 3 hours, and preferably overnight.

daisies

Tint some gum paste your chosen colour by gradually adding food colouring paste and kneading it in until completely incorporated. Very lightly dust the work surface with icing/confectioners' sugar and roll out some gum paste to a thickness of about 1 mm/¹⁄₃₂ inch. Using daisy cutters in assorted sizes, stamp out shapes from the gum paste and allow to dry on scrunched up parchment paper – this will give the flowers a shapely curl. Scoop 2 tablespoons of pre-made royal icing into a small bowl and tint yellow using food colouring paste. Spoon this into a disposable piping bag and pipe a yellow dot into the middle of each daisy. Allow to dry for at least 24 hours.

baby showers

You can buy almost anything to adorn a cupcake these days, but the best and prettiest things are often homemade. As you've gone to the trouble to make your own delicious cupcakes, I boldly suggest that you make your own cupcake picks to stick into them. All you need are a few basic craft materials, a small amount of creativity and a dash of imagination. Add to this some two-tone frosting which is easy to achieve and looks stunning. Look for disposable piping bags that are specially designed with this in mind – they have two pockets for the frosting and a clever nozzle/tip that is split in two, making it even easier to get picture-perfect results.

marbly swirl cupcakes

makes 12

1 quantity Vanilla Cupcakes (page 8)

1½ quantities Meringue Buttercream (page 12, but follow the method on this page)

pink and blue food colouring pastes

12-hole muffin pan, lined with pink and blue paper cases

2 large piping bags plus a large star-shaped nozzle/tip

12 baby-themed cake toppers, or to make your own, stamp/draw pictures onto craft paper, cut out and fold around the top of 12 cocktail sticks/toothpicks, then stick in place with glue

Preheat the oven to 180°C (350°F) Gas 4.

Prepare and bake the Vanilla Cupcakes as described on page 8.

Allow the cakes to rest in the pan for 3–4 minutes, then transfer to a wire rack and allow to cool completely.

Prepare the Meringue Buttercream as described on page 12 but I suggest that you make one quantity at a time rather than doubling up on the recipe and attempting to make it all at once. Not only will it be easier but it will be less tricky and messy – believe me, I've been there!

Divide the buttercream evenly between 2 mixing bowls. Cover one bowl with clingfilm/plastic wrap and set aside. Divide the other bowl of buttercream evenly in 2 again and using separate bowls, tint one half pink and one half blue using the food colouring pastes.

Fit one of the piping bags with the star-shaped nozzle/tip and lay the bag open on the work surface. Carefully spoon half of the white buttercream into the bag, trying to keep the buttercream smooth and into the bottom side of the bag. Carefully spoon the pink buttercream on top of the white in the bag so that when you pick the bag up, one side is filled with white buttercream and the other side is pink. Twist the end of the bag tightly so that there are no air pockets in the frosting and pipe a generous swirl on top of 6 of the cupcakes. The buttercream should come out of the piping bag in a swirl of pink and white loveliness.

Repeat this process with the remaining white and blue buttercream in another disposable piping bag fitted with the star-shaped nozzle/tip and pipe over the remaining cupcakes.

Push a cake topper into each cake to serve.

Battenburg is a much-loved classic British cake. In this recipe it's made in miniature, with each piece being just enough for a couple of bites.

baby battenburgs

makes about 24

150 g/10 tablespoons butter, soft and cubed

150 g/¾ cup (caster) sugar

3 eggs, lightly beaten

1 teaspoon pure vanilla extract

150 g/1 cup plus 2 tablespoons self-rising flour

a pinch of salt

2 tablespoons milk

pink food colouring paste

3 tablespoons apricot jam

350 g/12 oz. natural marzipan, divided in 4

20-cm/8-in. square cake pan, greased and lined with greased parchment paper

20-cm/8-in. square of foil folded in half and half again so that the strip is 20 cm/8 in. long with 4 layers of foil. Fold 2–3 mm/ ⅛ in. of the long edge back so that you have 2 little 'feet' opening out. Place across the middle of the prepared cake pan, 'feet' down, to divide the pan evenly

Preheat the oven to 180°C (350°F) Gas 4.

Cream the butter and sugar until pale, light and fluffy – about 3 minutes in a stand mixer. Gradually add the beaten eggs, mixing well between each addition. Add the vanilla and mix again. Sift the flour and salt into the bowl, add the milk and mix again until smooth and thoroughly combined.

Weigh the cake mixture and scoop half into one side of the prepared cake pan, spreading it level with a palette knife. Tint the remaining mixture pink using the food colouring paste and spoon into the other half of the pan, then spread it level. Bake on the middle shelf of the preheated oven for 15–20 minutes until well risen and a skewer inserted into the middle of the cake comes out clean. Allow the cake to rest in the pan for 3–4 minutes, then transfer to a wire rack and allow to cool completely.

Stack the cakes on top of each other and trim the sides with a long knife to make each cake the same size. (1)

Unstack the cakes and slice each in half horizontally. Lay the yellow cakes on the work surface, cut side up, and brush the top with apricot jam. Top each yellow cake with a pink cake and press gently together to make a stack. (2)

Cut each stack into 4 equal strips roughly 18 cm/7 inches long and roughly 2 cm/¾ inch wide. Starting from the left, flip the first strip over so that the yellow layer is on top. Repeat this step with alternate strips. Brush the inside of strip 1 with apricot jam and press together with strip 2. Repeat this with strips 3 and 4 and so on until you have 4 sections.

Lightly dust the work surface with icing/confectioners' sugar and roll out each piece of marzipan until about 20 cm x 16 cm x 2 mm/8 x 6½ x 1/16 inch. Brush with apricot jam. Neatly trim one long edge and place one cake section along this edge. Roll the cake in the marzipan to cover all 4 sides. Trim off any excess and repeat with the other sections. (3)

Cut into slices to serve.

Look for cute baby-themed cutters online or in bakeware stores – there's a varied and wonderful selection of shapes out there. These baby bottles are one of the simplest and here I've given instructions for an easy way to decorate them but feel free to further embellish the cookies with names, initials or shapes depending on your piping skills!

baby bottle cookies

makes about 16

1 quantity Vanilla Shortbread dough (page 10)

400 g/2⅔ cups royal icing sugar/ mix (or 2½ cups confectioners' sugar mixed with 2 tablespoons meringue powder)

pink and blue food colouring pastes

baby bottle cookie cutter

baking sheets, lined with parchment paper

disposable piping bags

Prepare the Vanilla Shortbread dough as described on page 10. Flatten the dough into a fat disc, wrap in clingfilm/plastic wrap and refrigerate until firm or for at least 2 hours.

Lightly flour the work surface and roll the dough out to a thickness of about 2 mm/ ¹⁄₁₆ inch. Using the cookie cutter, stamp out shapes from the dough and arrange on the prepared baking sheets. Gather the dough scraps together, press into a smooth-ish ball, re-roll and stamp out more cookies. Refrigerate the cookies for 20 minutes while you preheat the oven to 170°C (325°F) Gas 3.

Bake the cookies on the middle shelf of the preheated oven for about 12 minutes or until pale golden – you may need to swap the sheets around halfway through baking to ensure that the cookies brown evenly. Remove from the oven and allow to cool on the baking sheets.

To make royal icing, tip the royal icing sugar/ mix into a mixing bowl and whisk in enough cold water to make a smooth icing that will hold a ribbon trail when the whisk is lifted from the bowl. Spoon 2–3 tablespoons of the icing into a small bowl, and 2–3 tablespoons into another bowl. Tint one of the bowls pink and the other one baby blue using the food colouring pastes. Cover the bowls with clingfilm/plastic wrap and set aside.

Spoon 2 tablespoons of the white icing into a disposable piping bag and snip the very tip off the bag with scissors. Cover the remaining white icing with clingfilm/plastic wrap to prevent it drying out. Pipe a fine outline around the bottle section of each cookie. (See page 11 for instructions on flooding.) Spoon half of the blue icing into another piping bag and half of the pink into another. Pipe either blue or pink outlines around the bottle and cap sections of each cookie. Allow to dry for about 10 minutes.

Add another drop of cold water to the remaining white icing to make it slightly runnier. Spoon it onto the bottle section of the cookies within the icing outline. Use a mini palette knife, back of a teaspoon or a small knife to spread the icing in a smooth layer up to the outline. Repeat this process with the pink and blue icing in the cap sections. Allow to dry for about 1 hour. Wrap the piping bags in clingfilm/plastic wrap to prevent the icing drying out, as you will need them again.

Finally, pipe blue or pink outlines around each bottle, measuring lines across the bottles and details around the cap sections. Allow to dry for at least 3 hours, and preferably overnight, before serving.

These colourful buttons look wonderful in assorted colours and sizes and 'sewn' onto cards or tied together in stacks.

button cookies

makes about 30–40 depending on size

1 quantity Vanilla Shortbread dough (page 10)

300 g/10 oz. ready-to-roll royal icing/fondant/sugar paste

pink, blue and yellow food colouring pastes

icing/confectioners' sugar, for dusting

plain cookie cutters in assorted sizes

baking sheets lined with parchment paper

Prepare the Vanilla Shortbread dough as described on page 10. Flatten the dough into a fat disc, wrap in clingfilm/plastic wrap and refrigerate until firm or for at least 2 hours.

Lightly flour the work surface and roll the dough out to a thickness of about 3 mm/⅛ inch. Using the cookie cutters, stamp out rounds in assorted sizes – I find that 3–5-cm/1¼–2-inch cutters work well. Arrange the cookies on the prepared baking sheets. Gather the dough scraps together, press into a smooth-ish ball, re-roll and stamp out more cookies.

Using the blunt side of the cutters or the wide end of a piping nozzle/tip, press an indent into each cookie so that there is a rim about 3 mm/⅛ inch from the outside of the cookie edge. Using a skewer, make 2 or 4 holes in the middle of each cookie. (1)

Refrigerate the cookies for 20 minutes while you preheat the oven to 170°C (325°F) Gas 3.

Bake the cookies in batches on the middle shelf of the preheated oven for about 12 minutes or until firm and pale golden. Remove the cookies from the oven, allow to cool on the baking sheets for 2–3 minutes, then push the skewer into the pre-made holes so that you can easily push thread through them later. (2)

Divide the ready-to-roll icing equally into 3 and tint each one a different colour by gradually adding food colouring paste and kneading it in until completely incorporated. Lightly dust the work surface with icing/confectioners' sugar and roll the icing out to a thickness of 2 mm/1/16 inch. Using the cutters, stamp out rounds to match the size and number of the cookies. Very lightly brush the top of each cookie with cold water and lay an icing round on top. Press gently into place, then use the blunt side of the cutters or a piping nozzle/tip again to mark the indents into the icing. Push the skewer through the holes in each button. (3)

Allow the icing to dry for at least 2 hours, and preferably overnight, before serving.

These little cheesecakes are just enough for two or three bites and therefore not as overwhelming as a whole slice, which can be too rich especially if you are serving lots of other sweet nibbles. They have a sour cream topping and a raspberry baked into the middle, which cuts through the richness and sweetness just enough. If you don't have a mini cake pan, bake these cheesecakes in muffin pans lined with paper muffin cases.

New York cheesecake bites

makes 12

100 g/3½ oz. digestive biscuits/
graham crackers

35 g/2 tablespoons butter, melted

400 g/14 oz. cream cheese

2 large eggs

250 g/1 cup sour cream

125 g/⅔ cup (caster) sugar

1 teaspoon cornflour/cornstarch

1 teaspoon pure vanilla extract

finely grated zest and juice of
½ lemon

12 raspberries, plus extra to serve

icing/confectioners' sugar,
for dusting

non-stick 12-hole mini cake pan

Preheat the oven to 170˚C (325˚F) Gas 3.

Finely crush the digestive biscuits/graham crackers either by blitzing them in a food processor or bashing them in a sealed freezer bag with a rolling pin. Tip the crushed biscuits into a bowl, add the melted butter and mix until thoroughly combined.

Divide the crumbs evenly between the holes of the cake pan and press down lightly into the base so that they form an even, compact layer. (I find the easiest way to do this is to use a small spice jar that cunningly fits snuggly inside the cake pan holes rather than messing around with my fingers.) Bake on the middle shelf of the preheated oven for 5 minutes. Remove from the oven but leave the oven on.

Combine the cream cheese, eggs, 100 g/½ cup of the sour cream, 75 g/⅓ cup of the sugar and all the cornflour/cornstarch in a bowl and whisk until smooth. Add the vanilla, lemon zest and juice and whisk again to combine. Carefully divide the mixture between the holes of the cake pan and push one raspberry into the middle of each cheesecake.

Bake the cheesecakes on the middle shelf of the oven for 20 minutes or until only just set. Remove from the oven and allow to rest for 5 minutes. Leave the oven on.

Meanwhile, beat together the remaining sour cream and sugar. Carefully spoon this mixture on top of the cheesecakes and return to the oven for a further 5–7 minutes until set but not coloured.

Remove the cheesecakes from the oven and allow to cool completely before refrigerating until chilled.

To serve, carefully push each cheesecake out of the pan and decorate with raspberries. Dust with icing/confectioners' sugar.

I have made these meringues in miniature here – enough for one bite – which I think is ideal for an elegant tea party. If you like, you could try tinting the meringue blue but I find that they do look slightly wrong this colour. Why not try scattering the meringues with contrasting coloured sprinkles before baking?

meringues

makes about 30

300 g/1½ cups (caster) sugar

150 g/⅔ cup egg whites (about 4 large eggs)

a pinch of salt

pink food colouring paste

300 ml/1¼ cups double/heavy cream

sugar thermometer

2 large piping bags, fitted with large star-shaped nozzles/tips

2 solid baking sheets, lined with parchment paper

Preheat the oven to 110°C (225°F) Gas ¼.

Tip the sugar into a medium heatproof bowl and add the egg whites, salt and 1–2 tablespoons water. Set the bowl over a pan of simmering water – you want the bowl to fit snuggly over the pan without the bottom of the bowl coming into contact with the water. Whisk slowly with a balloon whisk until the sugar has completely dissolved.

Continue to whisk until the mixture turns from opaque to white and thickens enough to hold a ribbon trail; at this point the meringue should read 60°C/140°F on a sugar thermometer.

Quickly scoop the mixture into the bowl of a stand mixer (or use a mixing bowl and an electric whisk) and whisk on high speed for about 4 minutes until the meringue is very thick and glossy white.

Scoop half of the meringue into another bowl and tint it pink using the food colouring paste. Whisk the meringue until it is evenly coloured.

Spoon the pink meringue into one piping bag and the white into another. Pipe small swirls onto the prepared baking sheets and bake on the middle shelf of the preheated oven for 40–45 minutes, swapping the sheets around halfway through baking to ensure that the meringues cook evenly.

Turn the oven off and leave the door propped open with a wooden spoon. Allow the meringues to cool down inside for 20 minutes. Remove from the oven and allow to cool completely.

To serve, whip the cream until it holds a peak, then spread 1 teaspoon onto the flat side of half of the meringues. Sandwich with the remaining meringues and serve immediately before they soften.

makes 24

150 g/1 cup plus 2 tablespoons plain/all-purpose flour

½ teaspoon baking powder

2 tablespoons (caster) sugar

salt

75 g/5 tablespoons butter, chilled and diced

75 g/5 tablespoons cream cheese

50 g/½ cup ground almonds

1 egg yolk

1 tablespoon milk

12 big teaspoons raspberry jam

24 raspberries, to serve

filling

75 g/½ cup pine nuts

100 g/1 cup ground almonds

125 g/1 stick butter, soft

125 g/⅔ cup (caster) sugar

2 eggs and 1 egg yolk

3 tablespoons plain/all-purpose flour

1 teaspoon pure vanilla extract

finely grated zest of ½ lemon

2 x 12-hole bun pans, greased

8-cm/3-in. fluted cookie cutter

I do love frangipane, and I do love raspberries, and I do love delicate, dainty, girly pastries. Oh, look what we have here! All three in one little package. Cream cheese pastry is delightfully flaky, crumbly and rich and adds an extra whoop of richness to all pie crusts – not something that is strictly needed here, but what the heck...

raspberry almond tartlets

To make a pastry, tip the flour, baking powder, sugar and a pinch of salt into the bowl of a food processor. Add the butter and use the pulse button to blitz the butter into the dry ingredients until the mixture resembles fine sand. Add the cream cheese, ground almonds, egg yolk and milk and pulse again until the dough starts to come together. Tip out of the food processor into a mixing bowl and use your hands to bring the dough together into a neat ball, but do not overwork the pastry. Flatten into a disc, cover with clingfilm/plastic wrap and refrigerate for 1 hour.

After 1 hour, lightly flour the work surface, divide the dough in half and roll out one half to a thickness of about 2 mm/¹⁄₁₆ inch. Using the cookie cutter, stamp out as many rounds from the dough as you can and use to line the bun pans, gently pressing the dough into the holes of the pans with your fingers. Gather the dough scraps together and set aside while you roll out the second half of the dough and stamp out more rounds. Gather all of the dough scraps together and gently press into a ball. Re-roll and stamp out more rounds – you should aim for 24 in total. Refrigerate the dough-lined pans for 20–30 minutes while you prepare the filling and preheat the oven to 180°C (350°F) Gas 4.

To make the filling, tip the pine nuts onto a baking sheet and lightly toast in the oven for 4 minutes but keep an eye on them – they catch and burn in the blink of an eye. Remove from the oven and allow to cool completely.

Put the toasted pine nuts in the bowl of a food processor and blitz until finely ground. Add the almonds, butter and sugar and whizz again until thoroughly combined. Add the eggs, yolk, flour, vanilla, lemon zest and a pinch of salt and whizz until smooth. Spoon a big half-teaspoon of raspberry jam into the bottom of each pastry case and top with a dessertspoon of the filling mixture, spreading it to cover the jam.

Bake the tartlets on the middle shelf of the preheated oven for about 20 minutes until puffed up and golden brown. You may need to swap the sheets around halfway through baking to ensure that the tarts cook evenly. Remove from the oven and allow to cool in the pans for 4–5 minutes, then carefully transfer to a wire rack and allow to cool completely.

To serve, put a raspberry on top of each tartlet and dust with a little icing/confectioners' sugar, if you like.

Nothing says baby shower quite as much as these cookies do. Look for baby shower-themed cookie cutters in specialist bakeware stores or online – the choice is mind-boggling, but these strollers have to be my all-time favourite.

stroller cookies

makes 12–15

1 quantity Vanilla Shortbread dough (page 10)

500 g/3½ cups royal icing sugar/mix (or 3¼ cups confectioners' sugar mixed with 2½ tablespoons meringue powder)

pink food colouring paste

24 assorted small sugar flowers

10-cm/4-inch stroller-shaped cookie cutter

baking sheets, lined with parchment paper

disposable piping bags

Prepare the Vanilla Shortbread dough as described on page 10. Flatten the dough into a fat disc, wrap in clingfilm/plastic wrap and refrigerate until firm or for at least 2 hours.

Lightly flour the work surface and roll the dough out to a thickness of about 3 mm/⅛ inch. Using the cookie cutter, stamp out shapes from the dough and arrange on the prepared baking sheets. Gather the dough scraps together, press into a smooth-ish ball, re-roll and stamp out more cookies. Refrigerate the cookies for 20 minutes while you preheat the oven to 170°C (325°F) Gas 3.

Bake the cookies on the middle shelf of the preheated oven for about 12 minutes or until pale golden – you may need to swap the sheets around halfway through baking to ensure that the cookies brown evenly. Remove the cookies from the oven and allow to cool on the baking sheets.

To make royal icing, tip the royal icing sugar/mix into a mixing bowl and whisk in enough cold water to make a smooth icing that will hold a ribbon trail when the whisk is lifted from the bowl. Scoop two-thirds of the icing into a small bowl and tint pink using the food colouring paste. Cover this bowl with clingfilm/plastic wrap until ready to use. Spoon most of the white icing into a disposable piping bag and snip the very tip off the bag with scissors. Pipe a fine outline around the edge of each stroller hood, and pipe lines for the wheels and spokes. (See page 11 for instructions on flooding.) Fill another piping bag with most of the pink icing and pipe an outline for the body of the stroller. Allow to dry for 15–20 minutes. Wrap the piping bags in clingfilm/plastic wrap until you are ready to use them again.

Add a drop of cold water to the remaining white icing to make it slightly runnier. Spoon it onto the hood section of the cookies within the icing outline. Use a mini palette knife, back of a teaspoon or a small knife to spread the icing in a smooth layer up to the outline. Tint the remaining pink icing a different shade, add a drop more water and flood the body of the prams. Allow to dry for at least 30 minutes.

Use the remaining icing to pipe details, and embellish each wheel with a sugar flower. Allow to dry for at least 3 hours, and preferably overnight, before serving.

makes about 24

225 g/1¾ cups plain/all-purpose flour

½ teaspoon baking powder

50 g/⅓ cup custard powder

50 g/⅓ cup icing/confectioners' sugar

a pinch of salt

175 g/1½ sticks butter, chilled and diced

1–2 tablespoons milk

1 teaspoon pure vanilla extract

filling

50 g/1¾ oz. white chocolate, chopped

75 g/5 tablespoons butter, soft

50 g/⅓ cup icing/confectioners' sugar

1 tablespoon custard powder

1 teaspoon pure vanilla extract

assorted 5–6-cm/2–2¼-in. round or oval fluted cookie cutters

baking sheets, lined with parchment paper

Here's my take on a classic British teatime biscuit. I like to press patterns into the top of each cookie – similar to the original storebought versions – you could use letter and number cutters, or something as simple as the fine side of a grater. Look around your kitchen and you'll be surprised what you can use. I like to make my custard creams in very dainty little oval shapes – they look divinely elegant when packaged into little cellophane bags, tied up with pretty ribbons and given away as favours. If you like, you can also flavour the filling with a little melted milk chocolate.

custard creams

Sift the flour, baking powder, custard powder, icing/confectioners' sugar and salt into the bowl of a food processor and whizz for 30 seconds to combine. Add the butter and pulse until completely incorporated into the dry ingredients and it resembles dry sand.

Tip the mixture into a mixing bowl and make a well in the middle. Add the milk and vanilla and mix using a round-bladed knife until the dough starts to clump together. Use your hands to squeeze the dough into a smooth-ish ball but don't overwork it otherwise your cookies will shrink and toughen as they bake. Flatten into a disc, cover with clingfilm/plastic wrap and refrigerate for 30 minutes.

Preheat the oven to 170°C (325°F) Gas 3.

After 30 minutes, lightly flour the work surface and roll the dough out to a thickness of about 3 mm/⅛ inch. Using the cookie cutters, stamp out cookies in rounds and ovals and arrange on the prepared baking sheets. Gather the dough scraps together, press into a smooth-ish ball, re-roll and stamp out more cookies.

Create decorative patterns on each cookie by pressing something textured onto it, for example, I like to use the lemon zesting side of a box grater. Bake the cookies on the middle shelf of the preheated oven for about 10–11 minutes or until firm and very pale golden. Remove from the oven and allow to cool on the baking sheets for 3 minutes, then carefully transfer to a wire rack and allow to cool completely.

Meanwhile, prepare the filling. Melt the chocolate in a small heatproof bowl set over a pan of barely simmering water. Do not let the base of the bowl touch the water. Alternatively, melt the chocolate in a microwave on a low setting in short bursts. Remove from the heat, stir until smooth and allow to cool.

Beat the butter, sugar, custard powder and vanilla together until smooth, pale and light. Add the cooled, melted white chocolate and stir until smooth.

Spread the underside of half of the cookies with filling and sandwich with the remaining cookies.

Any afternoon party worth its towering cake stands nowadays includes a plate of French macarons. I prefer simple flavours and colours, so here I have opted for a raspberry and white chocolate, and lemon macaron.

macarons

makes 20–24

200 g/1⅓ cups icing/confectioners' sugar

100 g/1 cup ground almonds

1 tablespoon freeze-dried raspberry powder for raspberry macarons, or finely grated zest of 1 lemon and ½ teaspoon pure lemon extract for lemon macarons

125 g/½ cup egg whites (from roughly 3 large eggs)

a pinch of salt

40 g/5 tablespoons caster/superfine sugar

pink or yellow food colouring pastes

pink or yellow sugar sprinkles

white chocolate ganache (for raspberry macarons)

150 g/5 oz. white chocolate, finely chopped

5 tablespoons double/heavy cream

½ teaspoon pure vanilla extract

lemon cream (for lemon macarons)

150 ml/⅔ cup double/heavy cream

2 tablespoons lemon curd

large piping bag, fitted with a plain 1-cm/³⁄₈-in. nozzle/tip

2 solid baking sheets, lined with parchment paper or 2 silicone macaron mats

Tip the icing/confectioners' sugar, ground almonds and freeze-dried raspberry powder (for raspberry macarons) or lemon zest and lemon extract (for lemon macarons) into the bowl of a food processor and whizz for 30 seconds to thoroughly combine.

Put the egg whites in a large mixing bowl or the bowl of a stand mixer. Add the salt and whisk on medium speed until the egg whites are light and foamy. Gradually add the caster/superfine sugar 1 teaspoon at a time, mixing well between each addition. Continue whisking until the mixture is stiff and glossy and all of the sugar has been incorporated. Add a drop of pink or yellow food colouring and mix to thoroughly combine.

Using a large metal spoon or rubber spatula, fold the almond mixture into the egg whites. Continue to fold until smooth, shiny and the mixture is like molten lava.

Pour the batter into the prepared piping bag and pipe 20–24 even-sized macarons onto each baking sheet. Tap the sheets sharply on the work surface to knock out any air bubbles and scatter the tops of the macarons with pink or yellow sprinkles. Allow to rest for at least 15 minutes and up to 1 hour, by which time the surface of the macarons should be dry to the touch with a light skin on top.

Meanwhile, preheat the oven to 170°C (325°F) Gas 3.

Bake the macarons, one sheet at a time, in the middle of the preheated oven for 9–10 minutes or until the tops are firm and the macarons have risen. Remove from the oven and allow to cool on the baking sheets until completely cold and firm.

To make a white chocolate ganache, tip the chocolate into a small heatproof bowl. Heat the cream and vanilla in a small saucepan or in the microwave until just boiling. Pour the hot cream over the chocolate and allow it to melt for about 1 minute. Stir until smooth and allow to cool and chill until thickened.

To make a lemon cream, whip the cream until it will hold a peak, then fold in the lemon curd.

Spread ganache or cream over the underside of half of the macaron shells and sandwich with the remaining macaron shells.

If you have never tasted homemade marshmallows, then you have missed out on a real treat. They are enormously satisfying to make, deeply delicious and as light and airy as a pink sugar-cloud. They look beautiful in glass jars or packaged into cellophane or candy-striped bags and tied with pretty ribbons. The easiest way to make them is to scoop the marshmallow mixture into baking pans, allow to set, then cut it into squares. However, for an overload of 'wow' (and my preferred method, especially for girly gatherings), you can pipe the marshmallow into lengths using a piping bag and cut them into bite-sized pieces once set. Try flavouring your marshmallows with rosewater or lemon extract, if you like.

marshmallows

makes 30–40

2 tablespoons icing/confectioners' sugar

2 tablespoons cornflour/cornstarch

8 sheets of fine leaf gelatine

400 g/2 cups (caster) sugar

1 tablespoon glucose syrup/light corn syrup/golden syrup

2 large egg whites

a pinch of salt

1 teaspoon pure vanilla extract

pink food colouring paste

sugar thermometer (optional)

large piping bag, fitted with a large star-shaped nozzle/tip

2 large baking sheets, lightly greased with sunflower oil and lined with parchment paper

Mix the icing/confectioners' sugar and cornflour/cornstarch together in a small bowl and dust the prepared sheets with a thick, even layer, tipping out and reserving the excess.

Soak the gelatine leaves in a bowl of cold water while you continue with the recipe.

Tip the (caster) sugar and syrup into a medium saucepan and add 150 ml/⅔ cup water. Place the pan over medium heat and stir gently to dissolve the sugar. Increase the heat, pop the sugar thermometer into the pan and bring the mixture to the boil. Continue to cook at a steady boil until the syrup reaches 120°C (250°F) on a sugar thermometer, or until the syrup is at the 'hard ball' stage. Remove from the heat.

Working quickly, put the egg whites in the bowl of a stand mixer, add the salt and whisk until the egg whites will hold a stiff peak. Squeeze the excess water from the soaked gelatine leaves. Add them to the hot syrup and stir quickly until completely melted. With the motor running on medium speed, add the hot

syrup to the whisked egg whites in a steady stream. Add the vanilla and continue to whisk until the mixture is cool, very white and stiff enough to hold a firm ribbon trail when the whisk is lifted from the bowl. Add a tiny amount of pink food colouring paste and whisk until the marshmallow is evenly coloured.

Scoop the mixture into the piping bag and pipe thick lines across the prepared baking sheets, leaving space between each line. Allow to set for 10 minutes, then dust with some of the sugar-cornflour/-cornstarch mixture. Leave them in a cool place for at least 2 hours until firm and set.

When the marshmallows are completely set, dust the work surface or a large baking sheet with the reserved sugar-cornflour/-cornstarch. Carefully turn the marshmallow out onto the prepared surface and snip into bite-sized pieces using scissors or a large knife. Dust with more sugar-cornflour/-cornstarch to prevent the marshmallows sticking together.

This idea is possibly one of the simplest in my repertoire of iced cookies, requiring no food colouring or fancy, fiddly design. The footprint shape is quite easy to draw freehand but if you prefer you can cut out a paper template and lay this on the cookie and pipe the foot outline around it – just flip it over to make either left or right feet.

baby footprint cookies

makes about 24

1 quantity Gingerbread dough (page 10)

1 quantity Vanilla Shortbread dough (page 10)

400 g/2⅔ cups royal icing sugar/mix (or 2½ cups confectioners' sugar mixed with 2 tablespoons meringue powder)

10-cm/4-in. oval or round cookie cutter

baking sheets, lined with parchment paper

disposable piping bag

Prepare the Gingerbread and Vanilla Shortbread doughs, one at a time, as described on page 10. Flatten each dough into a fat disc, wrap in clingfilm/plastic wrap and refrigerate until firm or for at least 2 hours.

Lightly flour the work surface and roll one dough out to a thickness of about 3 mm/⅛ inch. Using the cookie cutter, stamp out shapes from the dough and arrange on the prepared baking sheets. Gather the dough scraps together, press into a smooth-ish ball, re-roll and stamp out more cookies. Repeat with the second dough. Refrigerate the cookies for 20 minutes while you preheat the oven to 170°C (325°F) Gas 3.

Bake the cookies on the middle shelf of the preheated oven for about 12 minutes or until pale golden – you may need to swap the sheets around halfway through baking to ensure that the cookies brown evenly. Remove the cookies from the oven and allow to cool on the baking sheets.

To make royal icing, tip the royal icing sugar/mix into a mixing bowl and whisk in enough cold water to make a smooth

icing that will hold a ribbon trail when the whisk is lifted from the bowl. Spoon 2–3 tablespoons of the icing into a disposable piping bag and snip the very tip off the bag with scissors. Cover the remaining icing with clingfilm/plastic wrap to prevent it drying out.

Pipe the outline of a baby's foot and toes onto each cookie, remembering that you will need an even number of left and right feet. (See page 11 for instructions on flooding.) Allow the icing to dry for about 10 minutes.

Add another drop of cold water to the remaining white icing to make it slightly runnier. Spoon it onto the foot and toe sections of the cookies within the icing outlines. Use a mini palette knife, back of a teaspoon or a small knife to spread the icing in a smooth layer up to the outline.

Allow to dry for at least 3 hours, and preferably overnight, before serving.

If you can, use large rather than small bear-shaped cookie cutters for these characters as it's easier to pipe a face on larger shapes. At home, I have a big box of ribbons in just about every colour and size imaginable. They seem to find uses in the funniest of ways and on this occasion the smaller pieces seemed perfect for making scarves for these little bears.

teddy bear cookies

makes 12–16

1 quantity Chocolate Shortbread dough (page 11)

400 g/2⅔ cups royal icing sugar/mix (or 2½ cups confectioners' sugar mixed with 2 tablespoons meringue powder)

brown food colouring paste

teddy-bear cookie cutter

baking sheets, lined with parchment paper

disposable piping bags

assorted ribbons

Prepare the Chocolate Shortbread dough as described on page 11. Flatten the dough into a fat disc, wrap in clingfilm/plastic wrap and refrigerate until firm or for at least 2 hours.

Lightly flour the work surface and roll the dough out to a thickness of about 2 mm/ ¹⁄₁₆ inch. Using the cookie cutter, stamp out shapes from the dough and arrange on the prepared baking sheets. Gather the dough scraps together, press into a smooth-ish ball, re-roll and stamp out more cookies. Refrigerate the cookies for 20 minutes while you preheat the oven to 170°C (325°F) Gas 3.

Bake the cookies on the middle shelf of the preheated oven for about 12 minutes or until firm. Be careful not to overbake the cookies – it's hard to tell how baked they are because of the darkness of the dough. Swap the baking sheets around halfway through baking to ensure that the cookies bake evenly. Remove the cookies from the oven and allow to cool on the baking sheets.

To make royal icing, tip the royal icing sugar/mix into a mixing bowl and whisk in enough cold water to make a smooth icing that will hold a ribbon trail when the whisk is lifted from the bowl. Use the brown food colouring paste to tint the icing teddy-bear brown. Spoon 2–3 tablespoons of the icing into another small bowl and

add a little extra brown colouring to make the icing a darker shade and a little more icing sugar/mix to thicken the icing to a piping consistency – it should hold a ribbon trail when the whisk is lifted from the bowl. Cover the paler brown icing with clingfilm/ plastic wrap to prevent it drying out. Spoon the darker icing into a disposable piping bag. Snip the very tip off the piping bag with scissors and pipe oval outlines for each bear's paws. (See page 11 for instructions on flooding.) Cover this bag with clingfilm/ plastic wrap. Spoon the paler icing into another piping bag and snip the very end off. Pipe an outline around the edge of each teddy bear. Cover the piping bag with clingfilm/plastic wrap and allow the cookies to dry for about 15 minutes.

Add another drop of cold water to the paler icing and spoon into the body of the bears within the outlines. Use a mini palette knife, back of a teaspoon or a small knife to spread the icing in a smooth layer up to the outline. Add a bit more food colouring paste to this icing to darken it, then use it to flood the paws. Allow to dry for at least 1 hour.

Finally, use the darker icing to pipe eyes, a nose and a mouth onto each bear. Allow to dry for at least 3 hours, and preferably overnight, before tying a small length of ribbon around each teddy's neck to serve.

 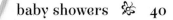

I have used a basic gingerbread-man cutter to make these babies and simply 'dressed' them in either pink or blue baby-grows. Gingerbread-men cutters come in a variety of sizes, so you could make a selection of different-sized babies and dress them in a rainbow of pastel baby-grows!

gingerbread babies

makes 12–16

1 quantity Gingerbread dough (page 10)

400 g/2⅔ cups royal icing sugar/mix (or 2½ cups confectioners' sugar mixed with 2 tablespoons meringue powder)

pink, blue and black food colouring pastes

gingerbread-man cookie cutter

baking sheets, lined with parchment paper

disposable piping bags

Prepare the Gingerbread dough as described on page 10. Flatten the dough into a fat disc, wrap in clingfilm/plastic wrap and refrigerate until firm or for at least 2 hours.

Lightly flour the work surface and roll the dough out to a thickness of about 3 mm/⅛ inch. Using the cookie cutter, stamp out shapes from the dough and arrange on the prepared baking sheets. Gather the dough scraps together, press into a smooth-ish ball, re-roll and stamp out more cookies. Refrigerate the cookies for 20 minutes while you preheat the oven to 170°C (325°F) Gas 3.

Bake the cookies on the middle shelf of the preheated oven for about 12 minutes or until pale golden – you may need to swap the sheets around halfway through baking to ensure that the cookies brown evenly. Remove the cookies from the oven and allow to cool on the baking sheets.

To make royal icing, tip the royal icing sugar/mix into a mixing bowl and whisk in enough cold water to make a smooth icing that will hold a ribbon trail when the whisk is lifted from the bowl. Spoon 1 tablespoon of the icing into a small bowl, cover and set aside. Divide the remaining icing between 2 bowls and

tint one bowl pale pink and the other baby blue using the food colouring pastes. Spoon 2 tablespoons of icing from each bowl into 2 smaller bowls and add a little more food colouring to each to make deeper shades of pink and blue. Spoon each darker icing into a disposable piping bag. Cover the pale icings with clingfilm/plastic wrap until ready to use.

Snip the very tip off each piping bag with scissors and pipe a fine pink or blue baby-grow outline around the body section of each gingerbread baby. (See page 11 for instructions on flooding.) Allow to dry for about 10 minutes and wrap the piping bags in clingfilm/plastic wrap.

Add a drop of cold water to the paler icings to make them slightly runnier and spoon the corresponding colour onto each cookie within the baby-grow outlines. Use a mini palette knife, back of a teaspoon or a small knife to spread the icing in a smooth layer up to the outline. Allow to dry for about 1 hour.

Finally, pipe fine details onto the baby cookies using the darker pink and blue icing. Using the reserved white icing, pipe tiny features onto each face. Allow to dry for at least 3 hours, and preferably overnight, before serving.

This is my take on the classic New York-Italian tricolour cookies, which are commonly white, red and green to match the Italian flag. They are really more cake than cookie and no less yummy for it, with a deep almondy flavour, apricot jam and a coating of chocolate. I have replaced the traditional almond paste or marzipan with ground almonds, as I find that storebought pastes can have too much sugar.

rainbow cookies

makes 16–25

175 g/1½ sticks butter, soft and cubed

125 g/⅔ cup (caster) sugar

75 g/½ cup icing/confectioners' sugar

3 eggs, beaten

1 teaspoon pure almond extract

grated zest of ½ lemon

125 g/1 cup plain/all-purpose flour

½ teaspoon baking powder

100 g/1 cup ground almonds

a pinch of salt

2 tablespoons milk

pink food colouring paste

3 tablespoons apricot jam

75 g/2½ oz. dark/bittersweet chocolate, chopped

75 g/2½ oz. milk chocolate, chopped

3 x 20-cm/8-in. square baking pans, greased and lined with greased parchment paper

Preheat the oven to 170°C (325°F) Gas 3.

Cream the butter and both sugars with an electric whisk or stand mixer until light and fluffy. Gradually add the beaten eggs, mixing well and scraping down the side of the bowl between each addition. Add the almond extract and lemon zest and mix again. Sift the flour, baking powder, ground almonds and salt into the bowl, add the milk and mix until smooth.

Weigh the mixture. Transfer one-third into one of the prepared baking pans and spread level with the back of a spoon. Tint the remaining mixture pale pink using the food colouring paste, but go easy on it as a tiny amount goes a long way, and at this stage the mixture needs to be pale and not shocking pink. Scoop half of this pink mixture (roughly 250 g/9 oz. but weigh it again to check) into the second baking pan and spread level. Add another drop of pink food colouring to the remaining batter to make it a deeper shade of pink and spread this into the third baking pan.

Bake the cakes on the middle shelf of the preheated oven for about 8 minutes or until set and a skewer comes out clean when inserted into the middle of the cakes. You may need to bake these cakes on 2 shelves, in which case use one just below the middle of the oven and one above and rotate the pans halfway through cooking. Remove from the oven and allow to rest in the pans for 2–3 minutes. Using the parchment paper to help you, carefully lift out the cakes, put onto wire racks and allow to cool.

Warm the apricot jam in a small saucepan to make it runny, then pass it through a sieve/strainer to remove any lumps. Flip the untinted cake over, peel off the parchment paper and spread a layer of the warm jam over it. Top with the paler pink cake, remove the paper, then spread jam over the top of the cake. Peel the paper off the darker pink cake and lay it, top side uppermost, on top of the paler pink cake. Cover with a sheet of parchment paper and a baking sheet, press the cakes together and set aside for a few hours for the flavours to mingle and the slices to meld together.

Melt both chocolates in a heatproof bowl set over a pan of barely simmering water. Do not let the base of the bowl touch the water. Alternatively, melt them in a microwave on a low setting in short bursts. Remove from the heat, stir until smooth and allow to cool slightly.

Remove the baking sheet and paper from the cake. Spread half of the chocolate over the top of the cake and refrigerate for 10 minutes to set. Lay a clean sheet of baking parchment over the top of the cake, cover with a baking sheet again and flip the cake over. Spread the remaining chocolate over this untinted side of the cake. Allow the chocolate to set.

To serve, trim the edges and cut the rainbow cookies into squares with a sharp knife.

To my mind, no tea party is complete without something chocolatey, and when I want something chocolately at teatime I generally think of brownies. These rich offerings are an altogether more sophisticated affair, with their nuggets of white chocolate and pistachios lurking within the dense chocolate, making them perfect cut into tiny squares for a baby shower. You could also serve them as a dessert with a scoop of vanilla ice cream.

double chocolate brownie bites

makes about 24

225 g/8 oz. dark/bittersweet chocolate, chopped

200 g/14 tablespoons butter, diced

125 g/⅔ cup (caster) sugar

175 g/¾ cup light muscovado or light brown sugar

4 eggs, beaten

1 teaspoon pure vanilla extract

125 g/1 cup plain/all-purpose flour

1 tablespoon unsweetened cocoa powder

½ teaspoon baking powder
a pinch of salt

150 g/5 oz. white chocolate, chopped into chunks

75 g/½ cup shelled, unsalted pistachios, roughly chopped

20 x 30-cm/8 x 12-in. baking pan, greased and lined with greased parchment paper

Preheat the oven to 170°C (325°F) Gas 3.

Tip the dark/bittersweet chocolate, butter and both sugars into a medium heatproof bowl set over a pan of barely simmering water. Do not let the base of the bowl touch the water. Allow the ingredients to melt, stirring from time to time. Once smooth, remove from the heat and allow to cool slightly. Alternatively, melt the mixture in a microwave on a low–medium setting in short bursts, stirring from time to time, then allow to cool slightly.

Gradually add the beaten eggs to the cooled mixture, whisking between each addition to combine evenly. Add the vanilla and mix again. Sift the flour, cocoa, baking powder and salt into the bowl and fold in using a rubber spatula or large metal spoon. Add the white chocolate and pistachios and mix to combine.

Pour the brownie mixture into the prepared baking pan, spread level with the back of a spoon or palette knife and bake on the middle shelf of the preheated oven for 20–25 minutes until the top is just firm. Remove from the oven and allow to cool completely in the pan.

To serve, cut the brownie into bite-sized pieces with a sharp knife.

This multi-layered cake is a vision in pink and white. Not only are some of the cake layers tinted a delicate shade of pink but half of the frosting is flavoured with delicious sweet strawberry purée. If you don't feel up to piping roses or rosettes on top of the cake, then simply use the extra frosting to fill the cake even more and perhaps top the cake with some extra strawberries.

pink & white layer cake

serves 10–12

175 g/1½ sticks butter, soft and cubed

225 g/1 cup plus 2 tablespoons (caster) sugar

4 eggs, beaten

1 teaspoon pure vanilla extract or vanilla bean paste

275 g/2 cups plain/all-purpose flour

2 teaspoons baking powder

½ teaspoon bicarbonate of/ baking soda

a pinch of salt

75 g/⅓ cup sour cream, at room temperature

2 tablespoons milk

pink food colouring paste

to fill and decorate

250 g/2 cups ripe strawberries

1 teaspoon lemon juice

2 teaspoons (caster) sugar

½ teaspoon pure vanilla extract or vanilla bean paste

1 quantity Meringue Buttercream (page 12)

pink and white sugar pearls

edible sugar flowers

3 x 18-cm/7-in. round cake pans, greased and baselined with greased parchment paper

piping bag, fitted with a large star-shaped nozzle/tip

Preheat the oven to 180°C (350°F) Gas 4.

Cream the butter and sugar with an electric whisk or stand mixer until really pale, light and fluffy – at least 3 minutes. Gradually add the beaten eggs, mixing well and scraping down the side of the bowl between each addition. Add the vanilla and mix again. Sift the flour, baking powder, bicarbonate of/baking soda and salt into the bowl, add the sour cream and milk and mix gently until silky smooth.

Weigh the mixture. Take two-thirds of the mixture and divide evenly between 2 of the prepared cake pans. Spread level with the back of a spoon. Tint the remaining mixture pink, spoon into the third cake pan and spread level.

Bake the cakes on the middle shelf of the preheated oven for 20–25 minutes or until well risen, golden and a skewer comes out clean when inserted into the middle of the cakes. Allow the cakes to rest in the pans for 5 minutes, then carefully turn out onto wire racks and allow to cool completely.

To make the strawberry filling, hull and halve the strawberries and tip into a saucepan with the lemon juice, sugar and vanilla. Cook over low heat until the juice starts to run from the berries. Continue to cook until the mixture has thickened and is jammy, stirring frequently to prevent the mixture sticking to the bottom of the pan. Remove from the heat and push the fruit through a fine nylon sieve/strainer to remove the seeds and set aside until completely cold.

Meanwhile, to decorate, prepare the Meringue Buttercream as described on page 12 and divide between 2 bowls. Fold the cold strawberry purée into one bowl of the buttercream until smooth and well combined.

Using a long, serrated knife, slice each of the cakes in half horizontally to make 6 layers of even thickness. Place one of the untinted cake layers on a serving plate and spread 2–3 tablespoons of the strawberry buttercream over the top. Top with a pink cake layer. Spread 2–3 tablespoons of plain buttercream over the top and top with another untinted cake layer. Repeat this layering until you finish with an untinted cake layer. You will have one pink layer left over with which you can make cake pops (page 107). Cover the top and sides of the whole cake with the remaining plain buttercream, spreading it smoothly with a palette knife.

Fill the piping bag with the remaining strawberry buttercream and pipe large rosettes on the top of the cake. Refrigerate for 15 minutes.

To serve, scatter sugar pearls over the top of the cake and arrange sugar flowers around the base.

'Millefeuille' means 'one thousand leaves' and this is what this classic French dish is said to resemble with its crisp, golden, multi-layered puff pastry. It is traditionally filled with crème pâtissière but I prefer this more summery version, with sliced strawberries and whipped cream – oh what's not to like?

strawberry cream millefeuille

serves 6–8

800 g/2 lb. ripe strawberries

juice of 1 lemon

2 tablespoons (caster) sugar

½ vanilla bean, split in half

500 g/1 lb. all-butter puff pastry

2 tablespoons icing/confectioners' sugar, plus extra for dusting

500 ml/2 cups double/heavy cream

baking sheets, lined with parchment paper

Hull and halve half of the strawberries and tip into a heavy-based saucepan with half of the lemon juice, the 2 tablespoons (caster) sugar and the split vanilla bean. Cook over low heat until the juice starts to run from the berries, stirring from time to time. Continue to cook until the mixture has thickened and is jammy, stirring frequently to prevent the mixture sticking to the bottom of the pan. Remove from the heat and push the fruit through a fine nylon sieve/strainer to remove the seeds and vanilla bean, then set aside to cool completely.

Lightly flour the work surface and roll the puff pastry out into a rectangle about 40 x 30 cm/16 x 12 inches, and about 3 mm/⅛ inch thick. Using a long, sharp knife, trim the edges of the pastry square, then cut it into 3 neat rectangles each measuring 28 x 12 cm/11 x 5 inches and carefully lift onto the prepared baking sheets. Prick the pastry all over with a fork and refrigerate for 30 minutes while you preheat the oven to 200°C (400°F) Gas 6.

Depending on the size of your baking sheets, you may need to bake the pastry one section at a time. Bake on the middle shelf of the preheated oven for about 10–12 minutes or until starting to turn golden brown at the edges. Remove from the oven, lightly dust the top of each pastry rectangle with icing/confectioners' sugar and lay a sheet of parchment paper and a similar-sized baking sheet on top. Continue to bake for a further 8 minutes until golden brown, remove the baking sheet and paper from the top, then bake for a further couple of minutes until the pastry is evenly browned, crisp and puffed. Remove from the oven and allow to cool on a wire rack.

Keep a small handful of the best-looking strawberries to decorate, then hull and slice the remainder.

Lightly whip the cream with the icing/confectioners' sugar until it will just hold a peak. Choose the most perfect pastry rectangle and set this aside to use as your top layer. Lay one of the other rectangles on a serving plate and using a palette knife, spread half of the whipped cream over the rectangle. Arrange half of the sliced strawberries on top and drizzle half of the reserved strawberry purée over those. Lay the second pastry rectangle on top and repeat this layering. Top with your reserved best pastry rectangle and arrange the prettiest strawberries around the millefeuille.

Dust icing/confectioners' sugar over everything to serve.

naming days & christenings

I have a very clever square baking pan for this recipe, cunningly divided into 16 squares making it oh-so-easy to create picture-perfect mini cakes. If you can't find one of these, use a regular square pan. I suggest making these the day before you plan to ice them to prevent too many fresh crumbs dropping into the icing.

coffee & hazelnut cakes

makes 16

100 g/²⁄₃ cup blanched hazelnuts

125 g/1 stick butter, soft

175 g/³⁄₄ cup plus 2 tablespoons golden caster or natural cane sugar

2 large eggs, beaten

175 g/1¹⁄₃ cups plain/all-purpose flour

1½ teaspoons baking powder

½ teaspoon bicarbonate of/baking soda

a pinch of salt

75 ml/¹⁄₃ cup buttermilk, at room temperature

3 teaspoons coffee essence

to fill and decorate

250 g/1³⁄₄ cups fondant icing sugar

4 teaspoons coffee essence

50 g/1³⁄₄ oz. dark/bittersweet chocolate, chopped

50 g/¹⁄₄ cup (caster) sugar

2 large egg yolks

1 teaspoon pure vanilla extract

150 g/10 tablespoons butter, soft

16-hole mini square baking pan, greased and lightly dusted with flour, or a 23-cm/9-in. square baking pan, greased and lined with greased parchment paper

Preheat the oven to 180°C (350°F) Gas 4.

Lightly toast the hazelnuts in a baking pan in the preheated oven for 5 minutes or until pale golden. Cool completely, then whiz all but 16 of them in a food processor until finely ground. Reserve the whole nuts for later. Leave the oven on.

Cream the butter and sugar with an electric whisk or stand mixer until really pale, light and fluffy – at least 3 minutes. Gradually add the beaten eggs, mixing well and scraping down the side of the bowl between each addition. Sift the flour, baking powder, bicarbonate of/baking soda and salt into the bowl, add the buttermilk, coffee essence and ground hazelnuts and mix again on low speed until smooth and thoroughly mixed. Spoon the mixture into the prepared baking pan, filling each hole (or the plain baking pan, if using) no more than half full. Bake on the middle shelf of the preheated oven for about 25 minutes until golden brown, well risen and a skewer inserted into the middle of the cake(s) comes out clean. Allow to rest in the pan for 5–10 minutes, then carefully turn out onto a wire rack and allow to completely. (If you have used a plain pan, cut the cooled cake into 16 squares.)

To decorate, sift the fondant icing sugar into a bowl, add half of the coffee essence and 1–2 tablespoons cold water and whisk until smooth and the icing will just hold a ribbon trail. Add more water or sugar to get the right consistency. To cover the top of each cake in fondant, either dip it in the icing and allow any excess to drip back into the bowl, or spoon the icing on top of the cake and spread it neatly to the edges. Allow to set for 30 minutes.

Melt the chocolate in a heatproof bowl set over a pan of barely simmering water. Do not let the base of the bowl touch the water. Remove from the heat, stir until smooth and allow to cool. Meanwhile, heat the (caster) sugar and 3 tablespoons cold water in a small pan over low heat until the sugar has dissolved. Bring to the boil and simmer for 1 minute until slightly thickened and syrupy. In a small bowl, whisk the egg yolks, vanilla and remaining coffee essence until combined. Pour the hot syrup onto the yolks in a stream, whisking constantly. Return the mixture to the pan and place over very low heat for 30–60 seconds, stirring constantly to cook the egg yolks without scrambling them. Scoop the mixture into a bowl and whisk until cool and thickened. Gradually add the butter, mixing well between each addition. Add half of the melted chocolate and stir until smooth.

Cut each cake in half horizontally and pipe rosettes of frosting onto the bottom half. Sandwich with the tops. Drizzle neat lines of the remaining chocolate over each cake and finish with a toasted hazelnut.

serves 12

500 g/1 lb. mixed dried fruit

1 star anise

½ vanilla bean

1 small cinnamon stick

4 cardamom pods, lightly bruised

250 ml/1 cup Earl Grey tea (made with
1 tea bag and boiling water)

1 strip of orange peel

1 big tablespoon (clear) honey

200 g/13 tablespoons butter, soft

200 g/1 cup packed light brown
(soft) sugar

3 large eggs, beaten

175 g/1⅓ cups plain/all-purpose flour

1 teaspoon baking powder

a pinch of salt

50 g/½ cup ground almonds

50 g/⅓ cup shelled unsalted pistachios,
chopped

50 g/⅓ cup blanched almonds, chopped

to decorate

4 tablespoons apricot jam

300 g/10 oz. natural marzipan

500 g/1 lb. ready-to-roll royal icing/
fondant/sugar paste

200 g/1⅓ cups royal icing sugar/mix
(or 1¼ cups confectioners' sugar mixed
with 1 tablespoon meringue powder)

green food colouring paste

1 Ladybug and several Daisies (page
13 – made 2 days in advance of cake)

*deep 20-cm/8-in. round cake pan, greased
and baselined with 2 sheets of greased
parchment paper*

disposable piping bag

I like to use soft prunes, apricots, Medjool dates, raisins,
sultanas and glacé/candied cherries for this take on
fruitcake. It is best made at least three days before serving
to allow the flavours to mature and can be made up to
three weeks in advance.

daisy chain cake

The day before you want to bake the cake, chop the larger pieces of dried fruit so that they are all roughly the size of a large raisin. Put all the dried fruit and whole spices in a large mixing bowl with the hot Earl Grey tea, orange peel and honey. Stir well, cover loosely with clingfilm/plastic wrap and allow to steep overnight.

The next day, preheat the oven to 150°C (300°F) Gas 2.

Stir the dried fruit and pick out the whole spices and orange peel. Cream the butter and sugar with an electric whisk or stand mixer until really light and fluffy – at least 3 minutes. Gradually add the beaten eggs, mixing well and scraping down the side of the bowl between each addition. Sift the flour, baking powder and salt into the bowl, add the ground almonds, nuts and plump dried fruit and stir well with a rubber spatula or large metal spoon until the mixture is smooth and all of the ingredients are thoroughly incorporated.

Spoon the mixture into the prepared cake pan and spread level with the back of a spoon. Bake in the bottom third of the preheated oven for about 2 hours or until a skewer inserted into the middle of the cake comes out clean. If the top of the cake is browning too quickly, cover it loosely with foil or parchment paper.

Allow to rest in the pan for at least 30 minutes, then turn out onto a wire rack and allow to cool completely before wrapping in parchment paper and clingfilm/plastic wrap. Allow to mature for at least 3 days.

To decorate, warm the apricot jam to make it runny, then pass it through a sieve/strainer to remove any lumps. Brush it over the top and side of the cake. Dust a work surface with icing/confectioners' sugar and roll out the marzipan to a disc 35 cm/ 14 inches across. Roll the marzipan up on the rolling pin and unroll over the cake to cover completely. Smooth the marzipan with your hands and trim off any excess from the bottom of the cake. Brush a little boiled water over the marzipan. Dust the work surface with a little more sugar, then roll out the ready-to-roll icing and cover the cake completely in the same way. Allow to dry for at least 2 hours.

Tip the royal icing sugar/mix into a bowl and whisk in enough cold water to make a smooth icing that will hold a ribbon trail. Tint it green using food colouring paste and spoon into a disposable piping bag. Pipe daisy stalks over the cake and arrange the Ladybug and Daisies along the stalks, pressing them into the icing to stick. Allow to dry before serving.

I have made these little treats in mini loaf pans because I love the idea of cakes for one. They work just as well in muffin pans, which should be greased and dusted with flour to stop the cakes sticking. Feel free to swap the coconut for ground almonds.

citrus coconut drizzle cakes

makes 8

175 g/1½ sticks butter, soft and cubed

175 g/1 scant cup golden caster or natural cane sugar, plus 5 tablespoons for the drizzle

2 eggs and 1 egg yolk, beaten

2 lemons

1 lime

175 g/1⅓ cups plain/all-purpose flour

2 teaspoons baking powder

a pinch of salt

50 g/½ cup desiccated coconut, plus 1 tablespoon for sprinkling

2 tablespoons milk or coconut milk

8 mini loaf pans, 10 x 5.5 cm/ 4 x 2⅛ in.

Preheat the oven to 180°C (350°F) Gas 4. Grease the mini loaf pans and line the base and ends with a strip of greased parchment paper.

Cream the butter and sugar with an electric whisk or stand mixer until really light and fluffy – at least 3 minutes. Gradually add the beaten eggs and yolk, mixing well and scraping down the side of the bowl between each addition.

Grate the zest from one of the lemons and the lime and add to the mixture. Sift the flour, baking powder and salt into the bowl, add the coconut and milk and mix gently until smooth.

Divide the mixture evenly between the prepared loaf pans and spread level with the back of a teaspoon. You may find it helpful to weigh the mixture to divide it super-evenly.

Bake on the middle shelf of the preheated oven for 18–20 minutes or until golden brown and a skewer inserted into the middle of the cakes comes out clean. Remove from the oven and allow to rest in the pans while you prepare the drizzle.

Squeeze the juice from both lemons and the lime and pour into a small saucepan. Add the 5 tablespoons of sugar and set the pan over low–medium heat to dissolve the sugar. Bring to the boil and boil hard until the syrup has reduced by half. Brush or spoon the warm syrup over the cakes (still in their pans), sprinkle 1 tablespoon coconut over the top and allow to cool completely.

These cakes keep really well for a couple of days in an airtight container.

These iced cookies are a touch nostalgic for me. As a child I loved anything decorated in feather icing, and I still do.

iced initial cookies

makes about 20

500 g/3½ cups royal icing sugar/mix (or 3¼ cups confectioners' sugar mixed with 2½ tablespoons meringue powder)

1 quantity Vanilla Shortbread dough (page 10)

flour, for rolling out

green and yellow food colouring pastes

disposable piping bags

non-stick parchment paper

8-cm/3¼-in. fluted cookie cutters in a variety of shapes

baking sheets, lined with parchment paper

The day before you want to bake the cookies, make the initials. Tip just less than half of the royal icing sugar/mix into a bowl and very gradually whisk in cold water until the icing is smooth, very thick, and will hold a firm ribbon trail when the whisk is lifted. Scoop into a disposable piping bag and snip the very tip off the bag with scissors. Pipe initials onto a sheet of non-stick parchment paper – you will need one for each cookie and they will need to fit in the middle of each cookie. Allow to dry for at least 24 hours. (**1**)

Prepare the Vanilla Shortbread dough as described on page 10. Flatten the dough into a fat disc, wrap in clingfilm/plastic wrap and refrigerate for at least 2 hours. After 2 hours, flour a work surface and roll the dough out until 2 mm/¹⁄₁₆ inch thick. Using the cookie cutters, stamp out as many shapes as possible and arrange on the prepared baking sheets. Refrigerate for 20 minutes and preheat the oven to 170°C (325°F) Gas 3. Bake the cookies on the middle shelf of the oven for about 12 minutes or until pale golden. Swap the sheets around halfway through to ensure even baking. Remove from the oven and allow to cool on the sheets.

Make up the remaining royal icing as above, but slightly runnier. Scoop 2 tablespoons into a disposable piping bag and cover the remainder with clingfilm/plastic wrap. Snip the tip off the piping bag and pipe an outline around the edge of each cookie. (See page 11 for instructions on flooding.) Allow to dry for 15 minutes. Divide the remaining icing between 2 bowls and tint one green and one yellow, adding a drop more water to make the icing slightly runnier. Spoon 2 tablespoons of each into separate piping bags and snip the tips off. Flood the cookies with one colour. (**2**)

Using the contrasting colour, pipe fine lines across each cookie. Drag a skewer through the lines of icing at 90°, first upward, then downward. Allow to dry for at least 1 hour. (**3**)

To serve, top each cookie with a prepared iced initial, stuck in place with a dot of royal icing.

This delicious nutty confection is perfect for an autumn celebration when summer berries are no longer in season and fruitcake seems too heavy. The cake layers keep for a couple of days in an airtight box, so you can prepare them ahead of time. Any surplus frosting can be piped as meringues and baked in a low oven for 45 minutes.

spiced maple syrup cake

serves 10–12

100 g/⅔ cup pecans, plus extra, chopped, to decorate

300 g/2⅓ cups plain/all-purpose flour

1 teaspoon ground cinnamon

a good grating of nutmeg

2 teaspoons baking powder

1 teaspoon bicarbonate of/baking soda

a pinch of salt

175 g/1½ sticks butter, soft

150 g/¾ cup (caster) sugar

100 g/½ cup pure maple syrup

1 teaspoon pure vanilla extract

3 large eggs, separated

200 ml/¾ cup buttermilk, at room temperature

gold sugar pearls

maple marshmallow frosting

150 g/⅔ cup pure maple syrup

3 large egg whites

100 g/½ cup (caster) sugar

a pinch of salt

3 x 20-cm/8-in. round cake pans, greased and baselined with greased parchment paper

sugar thermometer

Preheat the oven to 180°C (350°F) Gas 4.

Tip the pecans onto a baking sheet and lightly toast on the middle shelf of the preheated oven for about 5 minutes. Remove from the oven and allow to cool completely before blitzing in a food processor until finely chopped. Leave the oven on.

Sift together the flour, spices, baking powder, bicarbonate of/baking soda and salt and set aside.

Cream the butter and sugar with an electric whisk or stand mixer until really pale, light and fluffy – at least 3 minutes. Add the maple syrup and vanilla and mix for another minute or so. Add the egg yolks one at a time, mixing well and scraping down the side of the bowl using a rubber spatula between each addition. Whisk the egg whites in a clean bowl until they will just hold a stiff peak.

Using a large metal spoon or rubber spatula, fold the sifted dry ingredients into the creamed mixture in 3 batches, alternating with the buttermilk. Add the chopped pecans and mix to combine. Gently fold in the whisked egg whites trying not to knock out too much air.

Divide the mixture evenly between the prepared cake pans, spread level and bake on the middle shelf of the preheated oven for about 18 minutes or until golden, well risen and a skewer comes out clean when inserted into the middle of the cakes. You may need to swap the pans around halfway through baking to ensure that they cook evenly. Allow the cakes to rest in the pans for 3–4 minutes, then carefully turn out onto wire racks and allow to cool completely.

To make the maple marshmallow frosting, put the maple syrup in a small saucepan set over medium heat, bring to the boil and cook until reduced by half. Meanwhile, put the egg whites, sugar, salt and 1 tablespoon water in a heatproof bowl set over a pan of simmering water. Don't let the base of the bowl touch the water, but it should sit deeply into the pan so that half of the bowl is within the rim of the pan. Whisk the egg whites until the sugar has dissolved and the mixture starts to turn from opaque to white and thickens into glossy white clouds. Pour the boiling hot maple syrup into the egg whites, whisking constantly until glossy, smooth and the mixture reaches 60°C (140°F) on a sugar thermometer. Quickly scoop the mixture into the bowl of stand mixer and whisk on medium–high speed for about 3 minutes until cooled, thick and glossy.

Working quickly as the frosting sets as it cools, place one cake layer on a serving plate and spread a layer of frosting over the top. Cover with the second cake layer and more frosting. Finally, top with the third cake layer and cover the top and sides of the whole cake with the remaining frosting, using a palette knife to create generous swirls. Allow to set for 1 hour.

Decorate with pecans and gold sugar pearls.

These little floral delights wouldn't be out of place at the finest summer garden party. Feel free to make the flowers (a day in advance) in whatever shape or colour that takes your fancy – I think that simple, subtle and elegant is the way to go here.

pretty floral cupcakes

makes 12

150 g/5 oz. gum paste

green, lilac and pink food colouring pastes

1 quantity Vanilla Cupcakes (page 8)

½ quantity Meringue Buttercream (page 12)

300 g/10 oz. ready-to-roll royal icing/fondant/sugar paste

150 g/1 cup icing/confectioners' sugar, plus extra for rolling out

leaf sugarcraft cutters in assorted sizes

blossom sugarcraft cutters in assorted sizes

12-hole muffin pan, lined with pretty paper cases

fluted round cookie cutter, slightly wider than the widest part of the holes of the muffin pan (about 9–10 cm/4 inches)

disposable piping bag

The day before you want to bake these cakes, make the gum-paste flowers. Divide the gum paste equally into 3 and tint each a different colour by gradually adding food colouring paste and kneading it in until fully incorporated.

Lightly dust the work surface with icing/confectioners' sugar and roll out the green gum paste to a thickness of 1–2 mm/$\frac{1}{16}$ inch. Using the leaf cutter, stamp out as many leaves as possible in assorted sizes. Shape the leaves into elegant curls between your fingers and allow to dry on scrunched-up parchment paper to help them dry with kinks and curls.

Roll the lilac gum paste out to a thickness of 2 mm/$\frac{1}{16}$ inch and stamp out as many blossom shapes as possible in assorted sizes. Lightly crimp the edges of each blossom between your fingertips and allow to dry on the baking parchment. Lay a large sheet of clingfilm/plastic wrap on the work surface.

Break off pea-sized pieces of the pink gum paste and roll between your hands to make balls. Place on the clingfilm/plastic wrap and cover with another sheet. Using your thumb, flatten each ball until quite thin. Peel off the top sheet, take one disc and roll between your fingertips into a spiral to form the centre of a rose. Take another disc and wrap around the central one, covering the seam. As you add the petals, gently squeeze the edges to make them more curved. Continue until you have

a rose. Pinch off the excess gum paste from the bottom of each rose. Repeat to make lots more roses. Allow to dry overnight.

The next day, preheat the oven to 180°C (350°F) Gas 4.

Prepare and bake the Vanilla Cupcakes as described on page 8. Allow the cakes to rest in the pan for 3–4 minutes, then transfer to a wire rack and allow to cool completely.

Prepare the Meringue Buttercream as described on page 12 and spread smoothly over the top of each cupcake with a palette knife.

Tint the ready-to-roll icing a delicate shade of green by gradually adding the food colouring paste and kneading it in until fully incorporated. Lightly dust the work surface with icing/confectioners' sugar and roll out the green icing to a thickness of 2 mm/$\frac{1}{16}$ inch. Stamp out 12 discs using the cookie cutter. Lay a disc on top of each cake and gently smooth into place to completely cover the buttercream.

Mix the icing/confectioners' sugar with a little cold water until the icing will hold a ribbon trail. Tint this pink or lilac and spoon into a disposable piping bag. Snip the very tip off the bag with scissors and pipe a line of icing in delicate loops around the edge of each cupcake. Arrange the gum-paste flowers and leaves on top of each cake to serve.

Since childhood, I have been a big fan of iced buns – even as an adult
I can't resist it when I see a tray of them lined up in a bakery window.
With their slick of sweet icing and soft, light-as-a-feather crumb, what's
not to like? These little beauties are a little more special with their flourish
of sprinkles. Feel free to tint the icing in pale pastel colours, if you like, and
maybe split the buns in half and fill with piped whipped cream and jam –
but maybe I'm just getting carried away...

iced buns

makes 12

225 ml/1 scant cup full-fat milk

10 g/1 teaspoon active dry yeast

50 g/¼ cup (caster) sugar

450 g/3½ cups strong bread flour, plus extra for kneading

1 teaspoon salt

1 egg, lightly beaten

50 g/3 tablespoons butter, soft

sunflower oil, for greasing

300 g/2 cups icing/confectioners' sugar

food colouring pastes (optional)

assorted sugar sprinkles

2 baking sheets, lined with parchment paper

Heat the milk until it is hand-hot, by which I mean hotter than lukewarm but not hot-hot. Add the yeast and 1 teaspoon of the sugar and whisk to combine. Allow to rest for 6–8 minutes until the yeast has formed a thick foam on top of the milk.

Tip the flour into a large mixing bowl, add the remaining sugar and the salt and mix to combine. Make a well in the middle and add the milky yeast, egg and butter to the well. Mix with a wooden spoon and then your hands until the mixture comes together into a rough dough. Turn out onto a lightly floured work surface and knead for 5–10 minutes until the dough is soft, smooth and elastic. Alternatively, knead the dough using a stand mixer fitted with the dough hook attachment, in which case the kneading time will be less.

Wash and dry the mixing bowl and lightly grease with a little sunflower oil. Shape the dough into a smooth ball, place in the greased bowl and cover with clingfilm/plastic wrap. Leave the bowl in a warm, draught-free spot for about 1 hour or until the dough has doubled in size.

Tip the dough out of the bowl and onto a lightly floured work surface. Knead it for 30 seconds, then divide it into 12 equal pieces. Roll each piece of dough into finger shapes

or round buns. Arrange 6 buns on each of the prepared baking sheets, leaving plenty of space between each one. Cover loosely with clingfilm/plastic wrap and allow to rise for about 1 hour or until doubled in size and the dough springs back when gently pressed with your fingertip.

Meanwhile, preheat the oven to 190°C (375°F) Gas 5.

Bake the buns on the middle shelf of the preheated oven for about 15 minutes or until golden brown, swapping the baking sheets around halfway through baking to ensure that they brown evenly. Allow to cool on the sheets for 2–3 minutes, then transfer to a wire rack and allow to cool completely.

To make the icing, mix the icing/confectioners' sugar with 1–2 tablespoons cold water until it becomes a thick, spreadable paste. You don't want it too runny or it will slide off the top of your buns. If you fancied tinting the icing in various pastel shades, now is the time to do so using assorted food colouring pastes.

Spread some icing over the top of each bun and allow to set for 5 minutes before scattering sprinkles over them. Allow to set completely before serving.

For this recipe, I have added more glacé/candied cherries than you would usually get in a fruitcake and I've also added pecans, to complement them. I would suggest making these cakes a good couple of days before you plan to serve them and cover them with marzipan and icing the day before – this gives the flavours plenty of time to get to know each other.

mini fruitcakes

makes 12

125 g/1 cup mixed dried fruit

2½ tablespoons chopped candied peel

100 g/¾ cup glacé/candied cherries, rinsed and quartered

grated zest and juice of 1 orange

1 tablespoon brandy or whiskey

50 g/⅓ cup pecans, finely chopped

150 g/10 tablespoons butter, soft

100 g/½ cup light muscovado or light brown sugar

2 large eggs, beaten

1 tablespoon golden syrup or corn syrup

1 tablespoon treacle/dark molasses

150 g/1 cup plus 2 tablespoons plain/all-purpose flour

½ teaspoon baking powder

1 teaspoon mixed spice/apple pie spice

a pinch of salt

to decorate

2 tablespoons apricot jam

150 g/5 oz. natural marzipan

150 g/5 oz. ready-to-roll royal icing/fondant/sugar paste

24 Bootees (page 13)

non-stick 12-hole mini cake pan

fluted round cookie cutter, same diameter as holes of cake pan

ribbon, to decorate

Preheat the oven to 170°C (325°F) Gas 3.

Tip all the dried fruit, orange zest and juice, and brandy into a small saucepan and heat gently for 1 minute until the juice is hot but not boiling. Remove from the heat, add the pecans and allow to cool – the fruit will plump up and absorb the liquid. You can also heat the mixture in the microwave on a medium setting for about 1 minute, if you prefer.

Cream the butter and sugar with an electric whisk or stand mixer until really light and fluffy – at least 3 minutes. Gradually add the beaten eggs, mixing well and scraping down the side of the bowl between each addition. Add the syrup and treacle/molasses and mix well.

Sift the flour, baking powder, spice and salt into the bowl and fold in using a rubber spatula or large metal spoon. Add the dried fruit mixture and mix again to thoroughly combine. Divide the mixture between the holes of the cake pan.

Bake the cakes just below the middle of the oven for about 25 minutes or until well risen, golden brown and a skewer inserted into the

middle of the cakes comes out clean. Remove from the oven and allow to rest for 3–4 minutes, then carefully turn out onto a wire rack and allow to cool completely. Store the cakes in an airtight container until ready to decorate.

If the tops of the cakes are too domed, level them using a sharp, serrated knife.

Warm the apricot jam to make it runny, then pass it through a sieve/strainer to remove any lumps. Brush it over the top of each cake.

Dust a work surface with icing/confectioners' sugar and roll out the marzipan until it is about 2 mm/¹⁄₁₆ inch thick. Stamp out 12 discs using the cookie cutter. Lay a marzipan disc on top of each cake. Brush a little apricot jam over the marzipan discs. Dust the work surface with a little more sugar, then roll out the ready-to-roll icing until it is the same thickness as the marzipan. Stamp out 12 discs using the cookie cutter and lay one on top of each marzipan-covered cake. Press gently together. Allow the cakes to dry for about 2 hours.

Top each cake with a pair of Bootees and decorate with a ribbon, if you like.

No afternoon tea is complete without a tray of still-warm, crumbly scones with lashings of clotted cream and (preferably) homemade strawberry jam. Scones are one of the quickest and easiest teatime treats to make, however they do require a light touch as over-working the dough will result in tough, dry scones. The less you handle the dough the better the scones will be. There's only one real dilemma here – whether to put the cream or the jam on first.

buttermilk scones

makes about 12

450 g/3½ cups plain/all-purpose flour

2 teaspoons baking powder

a pinch of salt

100 g/7 tablespoons butter, chilled and diced

75 g/⅓ cup (caster) sugar

250 ml/1 cup buttermilk

1 egg white, lightly beaten

1 tablespoon granulated sugar

clotted cream or extra thick cream, and strawberry jam, to serve

medium round fluted cookie cutter

baking sheet, lined with parchment paper

Preheat the oven to 200°C (400°F) Gas 6.

Sift the flour, baking powder and salt into a large mixing bowl. Add the butter and 'cut' it into the dry ingredients using a round-bladed knife. Then use your fingers to rub the butter into the flour until it resembles fine breadcrumbs. Add the (caster) sugar and mix to combine.

Make a well in the middle of the mixture, add the buttermilk and stir in using the knife. Once the dough starts to come together, use your hands to shape it into a rough ball. Tip it onto the work surface and very lightly knead for 30 seconds or just long enough to make the dough almost but not quite smooth – lightness of touch is key here.

Lightly dust the work surface with flour and roll out or flatten the scone dough until roughly 2 cm/¾ inch thick. Using the cookie cutter, stamp out rounds and arrange on the prepared baking sheet. Gather the dough scraps together, press into a smooth-ish ball, re-roll and stamp out more scones. Brush the top of each scone with a little of the egg white, scatter granulated sugar over them and bake on the middle shelf of the preheated oven for about 10 minutes or until well risen and golden brown.

Transfer the scones to a wire rack and serve still ever-so-slightly warm from the oven and most certainly on the day of making.

To serve, split the scones in half and dollop a generous spoonful of jam on the cut side of each half, then top with cream.

These buttery, crumbly, vanilla-scented biscuits really do have to be piped into elegant shapes for full effect. I have coated the underside of each cookie in chocolate but you could just as easily dip the ends of each cookie into melted chocolate if you prefer. I decided that dark chocolate was too bitter and milk chocolate too sweet for these delicate bites and so struck a compromise between the two by using half and half. The extra sprinkles are perhaps not entirely necessary but elevate the swirls to a more girly high I think.

Viennese fingers

makes about 15

125 g/1 stick butter, soft

40 g/⅓ cup icing/confectioners' sugar

1 teaspoon pure vanilla extract

125 g/1 cup plain/all-purpose flour

2 tablespoons cornflour/ cornstarch

¼ teaspoon baking powder

a pinch of salt

50 g/1¾ oz. each dark/ bittersweet and milk chocolate, chopped (or all white chocolate if you prefer)

sugar sprinkles

piping bag, fitted with a large star-shaped nozzle/tip

baking sheet, lined with parchment paper

Preheat the oven to 170°C (325°F) Gas 3.

Cream the butter, sugar and vanilla with an electric whisk or stand mixer until pale and light – about 2 minutes. Sift the flour, cornflour/ cornstarch, baking powder and salt into the bowl and gently mix again until smooth and thoroughly combined.

Spoon the dough into the piping bag and pipe tight S-shaped spirals onto the prepared baking sheet. Bake on the middle shelf of the preheated oven for 10–12 minutes or until pale golden.

Remove the cookies from the oven and allow to cool on the baking sheet for 5 minutes, then carefully transfer to a wire rack using a palette knife or fish slice and allow to cool completely.

Melt both chocolates together in a heatproof bowl set over a pan of barely simmering water. Do not let the base of the bowl touch the water. Alternatively, melt them in a microwave on a low setting in short bursts. Remove from the heat, stir until smooth and allow to cool slightly.

Dip the underside of each cooled cookie into the melted chocolate, scatter sprinkles over the chocolate-coated edges and allow to set on baking parchment before serving.

I love all things sweet, miniature and baked. And I don't know anyone that doesn't like good old Victoria sandwich – so this recipe makes me a very happy person. These little classic cakes are enough for a couple of bites – any less just wouldn't be enough but they are also small enough that you can eat two without appearing too greedy! I know that it's not 100% traditional to fill Victoria sandwiches with buttercream as well as jam but I can't think of a good enough reason not to. If you don't have a mini cake pan, then simply use a trusty muffin pan greased with butter and dusted with a little flour.

mini Victoria sandwiches

makes 12

175 g/1½ sticks butter, soft and cubed

175 g/¾ cup plus 2 tablespoons (caster) sugar

3 large eggs, beaten

1 teaspoon pure vanilla extract

175 g/1⅓ cups self-raising flour

a pinch of salt

raspberry or strawberry jam, for filling

buttercream

150 g/10 tablespoons butter, soft and cubed

300 g/2 cups icing/confectioners' sugar, sifted, plus extra for dusting

1 teaspoon pure vanilla extract

non-stick 12-hole mini cake pan, greased

Preheat the oven to 180°C (350°F) Gas 4.

Cream the butter and sugar with an electric whisk or stand mixer until really pale, light and fluffy – at least 3 minutes. Gradually add the beaten eggs, mixing well and scraping down the side of the bowl between each addition. Add the vanilla and mix again.

Sift the flour and salt into the bowl and fold in using a large metal spoon or rubber spatula until the mixture is glossy and smooth.

Divide the mixture between the holes of the cake pan and spread level with a teaspoon. Bake on the middle shelf of the preheated oven for about 15 minutes until golden, well risen and a skewer inserted into the middle of the cakes comes out clean. Remove from the oven and allow to rest for 2 minutes, then carefully turn out onto a wire rack and allowing to cool completely.

To make the buttercream, beat together the butter, sugar and vanilla until pale and light.

Cut each cake in half horizontally and spread some buttercream over the cut side of the bottom half. Top with a teaspoon of jam and sandwich with the top half of the cake. Lightly dust with icing/confectioners' sugar to serve.

I recommend making the cake and praline the day before you plan to decorate and serve this. Decorate it with edible flowers, if you fancy!

chocolate & almond torte

serves 10

125 g/4 oz. dark/bittersweet chocolate, chopped

125 g/1 stick butter, soft and cubed

75 g/⅓ cup packed light brown (soft) sugar

75 g/⅓ cup (caster) sugar

3 eggs, beaten

1 teaspoon pure vanilla extract

75 g/⅔ cup plain/all-purpose flour

1 tablespoon unsweetened cocoa powder

75 g/¾ cup ground almonds

½ teaspoon baking powder

½ teaspoon bicarbonate of/baking soda

a pinch of salt

2 tablespoons sour cream

3 tablespoons boiling water

1 quantity Chocolate Ganache (page 12)

150 ml/⅔ cup double/heavy cream

2–3 tablespoons apricot jam

praline

75 g/⅓ cup (caster) sugar

75 g/½ cup blanched almonds

a pinch of salt

Swiss/jelly roll pan or baking pan, 33 x 23 cm/13 x 9 in., greased and lined with greased parchment paper

baking sheet, lined with non-stick parchment paper

piping bag, fitted with a star-shaped nozzle/tip

Preheat the oven to 180°C (350°F) Gas 4.

Melt the chocolate in a heatproof bowl set over a pan of barely simmering water. Do not let the base of the bowl touch the water. Remove from the heat, stir until smooth and allow to cool slightly.

Cream the butter and both sugars with an electric whisk or stand mixer until really pale, light and fluffy – at least 3 minutes. Gradually add the beaten eggs, mixing well and scraping down the side of the bowl between each addition. Add the vanilla and melted chocolate and mix again. Sift the flour, cocoa, ground almonds, baking powder, bicarbonate of/baking soda and salt into the bowl and mix until barely combined. Add the sour cream and boiling water and mix slowly until the mixture is silky smooth. Spoon into the prepared baking pan and spread level. Bake on the middle shelf of the preheated oven for 25 minutes or until a skewer inserted into the middle of the cake comes out clean. Remove the cake from the oven and allow to cool in the pan sitting on a wire rack.

To make the praline, put 2 tablespoons water and the sugar in a medium, non-stick frying pan over low heat. Heat until the sugar has dissolved, then increase the heat and bring the syrup to the boil, brushing the sides of the pan with warm water if the sugar starts to crystallize at the edges. Continue to boil until the syrup turns pale golden amber. Add the almonds and salt to the pan, stirring well to coat the nuts in the caramel. Cook for a further minute until the caramel is medium amber and the nuts are golden. Quickly tip the mixture out of the pan and onto the prepared baking sheet.

Do not stick your fingers into this hot caramel – it will hurt! Spread the praline in an even layer and allow to cool. Break the cold, hard caramel into chunks and whizz in the food processor until finely chopped.

Prepare the Chocolate Ganache as described on page 12 and allow to cool until thick enough to spread. Whip the double/heavy cream until it will just hold a stiff peak. Warm the apricot jam and strain to remove any lumps.

Carefully turn the cake out of the pan onto a tray or baking sheet, peel off the paper, lay another tray on top and turn it the right way up again. Using a long knife, trim the edges of the cake, then cut it into 3 equal rectangles each roughly 10 x 20 cm/4 x 8 inches. Place one rectangle on a serving plate and brush warm apricot jam over the top. Spread 2 tablespoons ganache smoothly over the jam and top with 1 tablespoon of the praline. Press the praline into the ganache and cover with half of the whipped cream. Top with the second layer and repeat the filling layers. Place the third cake layer on top, upside down, and very gently press down. Brush more jam over the top and sides of the whole cake and refrigerate for 10 minutes.

Coat the top and sides of the cake in all but 3 tablespoons of the remaining ganache. Press the remaining praline onto the sides of the cake. Pipe rosettes across the top of the cake with the remaining ganache and refrigerate for 20 minutes before serving.

baby birthdays

To make a birthday cake in the shape of a 1, 2 or 3, you don't need any specially shaped cake pans. Use a large rectangular pan and cut it into any number you like, then any off-cuts can be used to make Cake Pops (page 107). I decorated the three cakes on the following pages prettily but with minimum effort: frosting rosettes, pre-made icing shapes or simply a mass of candies and sprinkles.

first birthday cakes

serves about 20

350 g/3 sticks butter, soft

350 g/1¾ cups (caster) sugar

6 large eggs, beaten

2 teaspoons pure vanilla extract

350 g/2¾ cups plain/all-purpose flour

3 teaspoons baking powder

1 teaspoon bicarbonate of/baking soda

a pinch of salt

5 tablespoons buttermilk, at room temperature

to decorate

ready-to-roll royal icing/fondant/ sugar paste

6 tablespoons jam (apricot, raspberry or strawberry)

1 quantity Meringue Buttercream (page 12)

food colouring pastes

assorted candies and sprinkles

candles

33 x 23 x 6-cm/13 x 9 x 2¼-in. baking pan, greased and lined with greased parchment paper

piping bag, fitted with a star-shaped nozzle/tip

If you have the time, start the cake the day before you want to serve it. First, make any ready-roll-icing shapes, such as butterflies and numbers, that you need to decorate the cake.

Preheat the oven to 180°C (350°F) Gas 4.

Cream the butter and sugar until pale, light and fluffy – about 3 minutes in a stand mixer. Gradually add the beaten eggs, mixing well and scraping down the side of the bowl between each addition. Add the vanilla and mix again.

Sift the flour, baking powder, bicarbonate of/baking soda and salt into the bowl, add the buttermilk and either mix in the mixer or fold in using a rubber spatula or a large metal spoon. Once the mixture is smooth, spoon it into the prepared baking pan and spread level with the back of a spoon or a palette knife.

Bake the cake just below the middle of the preheated oven for 40–45 minutes until the cake is golden, well risen and a skewer inserted into the middle of the cake comes out clean. Allow the cake to rest in the pan for about 10 minutes, then turn out onto a wire rack and allow to cool completely.

Once the cake is cold, wrap it in clingfilm/plastic wrap until you are ready to finish the decorations. If you don't have time to leave the cake to the next

day before decorating it, pop it into the freezer for 20 minutes before cutting the number out. This will help stop too many crumbs from getting in the way of the frosting when you cut it up.

Cut a sheet of parchment paper to the same size as the top of the cake (use the baking pan as a guide) and draw number 1, 2 or 3 on the paper using as much of the area as you can. Cut out the number template. Place the cake on your serving plate and lay the template on top. Using a small, sharp knife cut the cake around the template. Save any cake trimmings to make Cake Pops (see page 107).

Warm the jam in a small saucepan to make it runny, then pass it through a sieve/strainer to remove any lumps. Brush the warm jam all over the top and sides of the cake in an even layer and allow to cool for 20 minutes.

Prepare the Meringue Buttercream as described on page 12. Spread two-thirds all over the top and sides of the cake in an even layer using a palette knife. Tint the remaining buttercream using food colouring paste, spoon into the piping bag and pipe shells or rosettes around or across the cake.

Decorate with candies, sprinkles and any icing shapes you have made.

This cake has a subtle malted chocolate flavour, and with six layers of cake and frosting it does look rather fabulous when cut into slices. If you prefer, however, you could assemble the cake as a three-layer confection but it does have a 'look-at-me' quality with six fabulous layers. If possible, the candle cookies should be baked and iced the day before you plan to serve the cake and put into position just before serving.

malted milk chocolate cake
with candle cookies

serves 12

175 g/1½ sticks butter, soft

225 g/1 cup plus 2 tablespoons (caster) sugar

3 large eggs, beaten

1 teaspoon pure vanilla extract

225 g/1¾ cups plain/all-purpose flour

2 teaspoons baking powder

½ teaspoon bicarbonate of/baking soda

30 g/¼ cup malted milk powder

2 tablespoons unsweetened cocoa powder

a pinch of salt

4 tablespoons buttermilk, at room temperature

75 ml/⅓ cup boiling water

½ quantity Vanilla Shortbread dough (page 10)

3 x 18-cm/7-in. round cake pans, greased and baselined with greased parchment paper

candle-shaped cookie cutter

baking sheets, lined with parchment paper

note: *turn to page 86 for decoration ingredients*

Preheat the oven to 180°C (350°F) Gas 4.

Cream the butter and sugar with an electric whisk or stand mixer until really pale, light and fluffy – at least 3 minutes. Gradually add the beaten eggs, mixing well and scraping down the side of the bowl between each addition. Add the vanilla and mix again. Sift the flour, baking powder, bicarbonate of/baking soda, milk powder, cocoa and salt into the bowl, add the buttermilk and mix gently until just combined.

Add the boiling water and mix again until the batter is silky smooth. Divide the mixture evenly between the prepared cake pans and spread level with the back of a spoon. Bake the cakes on the middle shelf of the preheated oven for 20–25 minutes or until well risen, golden and a skewer comes out clean when inserted into the middle of the cakes. Allow the cakes to rest in the pans for 10 minutes, then carefully turn out onto wire racks and allow to cool completely.

Prepare the Vanilla Shortbread dough as described on page 10. Flatten the dough into a fat disc, wrap in clingfilm/plastic wrap and refrigerate until firm or for at least 2 hours.

Lightly flour the work surface and roll the dough out to a thickness of about 2 mm/ ¹⁄₁₆ inch. Using the cookie cutter, stamp out shapes from the dough and arrange on the prepared baking sheets. Gather the dough scraps together, press into a smooth-ish ball, re-roll and stamp out more cookies. You will need 16–20 candle cookies to go around the cake. (*See picture 1, overleaf*)

Refrigerate the cookies for 20 minutes while you preheat the oven to 170°C (325°F) Gas 3.

Bake the cookies on the middle shelf of the preheated oven for about 12 minutes or until pale golden – you may need to swap the sheets around halfway through baking to ensure that the cookies brown evenly. Remove from the oven and allow to cool on the baking sheets. *Now turn to page 86.*

malted milk chocolate cake decoration

to decorate the cookies and cake

400 g/2⅔ cups royal icing sugar/mix (or 2½ cups confectioners' sugar mixed with 2 tablespoons meringue powder)

pink, blue and yellow food colouring pastes

100 g/3½ oz. dark/bittersweet chocolate, chopped

1 quantity Meringue Buttercream (page 12)

sugar sprinkles

disposable piping bags

To decorate the cookies, make a royal icing. Tip the royal icing sugar/mix into a mixing bowl and whisk in enough cold water to make a smooth icing that will hold a ribbon trail when the whisk is lifted from the bowl. Spoon 2–3 tablespoons of the icing into a disposable piping bag and snip the very tip off the bag with scissors. Pipe a fine outline around the body of each cookie, ie missing out the flame. (See page 11 for instructions on flooding.) Allow to dry for 15 minutes. Add another drop of cold water to the remaining white icing to make it slightly runnier. Spoon it onto the body of the cookies within the icing outline. Use a mini palette knife, back of a teaspoon or a small knife to spread the icing in a smooth layer up to the outline. **(2)**

Cover the remaining icing with clingfilm/plastic wrap to prevent the icing drying out, as you will need it again. Allow the candle cookies to dry for about 1 hour.

Tint 2–3 tablespoons of the remaining icing blue or pink using the food colouring paste and add a little more icing sugar/mix to thicken to a piping consistency. Spoon into another disposable piping bag and snip the very tip off the bag with scissors. Pipe a fine outline and details on the iced body of each candle. **(3)**

Tint the remaining icing yellow and pipe a flame outline onto each candle. Allow to dry for 10 minutes, then flood the outlines with yellow icing. Allow to dry for at least 3 hours, and preferably overnight (covered), before serving. **(4)**

To assemble the cake, melt the chocolate in a heatproof bowl set over a pan of barely simmering water. Do not let the base of the bowl touch the water. Remove from the heat, stir until smooth and allow to cool slightly.

Prepare the Meringue Buttercream as described on page 12. Scoop one-quarter into a smaller bowl and set aside. Add the melted chocolate to the larger quantity of buttercream and mix to thoroughly combine.

Using a long, serrated knife, slice each of the cakes in half horizontally to make 6 layers of even thickness. Place one of the bottom cake layers on a serving plate and spread one-third of the plain buttercream over it. Top with a second cake layer and spread a thin layer of chocolate buttercream over it. Repeat this alternate layering until you have 6 layers of cake, 3 layers of vanilla buttercream and 2 layers of chocolate buttercream. Cover the top and sides of the cake with the remaining chocolate buttercream, spreading it evenly with a palette knife. Scatter sprinkles over the top and refrigerate for 30 minutes. Press the candle cookies around the outside of the cake just before serving.

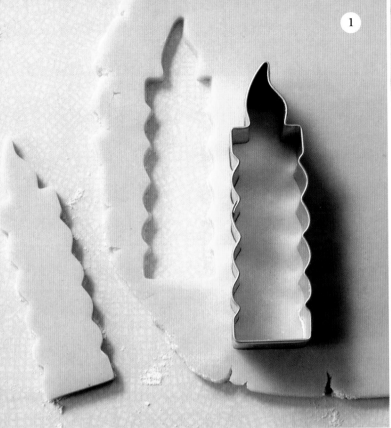

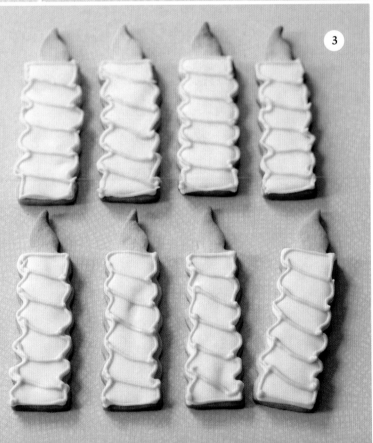

Everything you need to make these cute teddy bears can be found in the baking or confectionery aisle of the supermarket. Kids love them and they'll get particularly excited if you let them stick the decorations on at the end to make the teddy bears' faces.

teddy bear cupcakes

makes 12

1 quantity Chocolate Cupcakes (page 9)

1 quantity Chocolate Meringue Buttercream (page 12)

chocolate sprinkles or finely grated chocolate

24 giant milk chocolate buttons

24 white chocolate buttons

12 regular milk chocolate buttons

36 brown candy-coated chocolate drops

1 tube of chocolate writing icing or 50 g/1¾ oz. dark/bittersweet chocolate, melted

12-hole muffin pan, lined with brown paper cases

Preheat the oven to 180°C (350°F) Gas 4.

Prepare and bake the Chocolate Cupcakes as described on page 9. Allow the cakes to rest in the pan for 3–4 minutes, then transfer to a wire rack and allow to cool completely.

Prepare the Chocolate Meringue Buttercream as described on page 12. Using a small palette knife, cover the top of each cooled cupcake with chocolate meringue buttercream and scatter an even layer of chocolate sprinkles or grated chocolate over the top to resemble fur.

Lay the giant chocolate buttons on the work surface and dab the top of each with a dot of buttercream. Lay the white buttons on top and press together. Position 2 pairs of buttons at the top of each cupcake for ears.

Lay the regular milk chocolate buttons on the work surface, dab the underside of 12 of the chocolate drops with buttercream and press one onto each of the chocolate buttons. Dab a little more buttercream on the underside of each button and position as a nose on the cupcakes. Position the remaining chocolate drops as eyes and use the writing icing (or melted chocolate) to draw a mouth. Your teddies are now ready to serve.

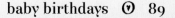

makes 12

175 g/1½ sticks butter, soft

175 g/¾ cup plus 2 tablespoons (caster) sugar

3 large eggs, beaten

1 teaspoon pure vanilla extract

175 g/1⅓ cups self-raising flour

a pinch of salt

½ quantity Meringue Buttercream (page 12)

6 teaspoons lemon curd or raspberry jam

assorted sugar sprinkles

icing/confectioners' sugar, for dusting

12-hole muffin pan, lined with pretty paper cases

large piping bag, fitted with a star-shaped nozzle/tip

There's no such thing as a children's party without a tray of butterfly cakes, in my opinion. If you are not so confident in your cake decorating skills, then these are the go-to option, guaranteed to bring a smile to the faces of adults and children alike. There's something nostalgic about butterfly cakes that will continue to make them a party favourite for years to come I'm sure. If you don't feel like making buttercream, try filling the cakes with a small dollop of jam or lemon curd and then topping with a swirl of whipped cream.

butterfly cakes

Preheat the oven to 180°C (350°F) Gas 4.

Cream the butter and sugar until pale, light and fluffy – about 3 minutes in a stand mixer. Gradually add the beaten eggs, mixing well and scraping down the side of the bowl between each addition. Add the vanilla and mix again.

Sift the flour and salt into the bowl and fold into the mixture using a large metal spoon or rubber spatula until the mixture is glossy and smooth.

Divide the mixture evenly between the paper cases and bake on the middle shelf of the preheated oven for about 15–20 minutes or until the cakes are golden, well risen and a skewer inserted into the middle of the cakes comes out clean.

Allow the cupcakes to rest in the pan for 3–4 minutes, then transfer to a wire rack and allow to cool completely.

Prepare the Meringue Buttercream as described on page 12 and spoon into the piping bag. Using a small, sharp knife, cut a cone shape from the top of each cupcake and set aside. Spoon half a teaspoon of lemon curd or jam into the hole in each cake and pipe a generous swirl of buttercream on top, filling the hole. Scatter the sugar sprinkles on top. Cut each of the reserved cake cones in half vertically and position in the buttercream to resemble butterfly wings. Lightly dust the cakes with icing/confectioners' sugar to serve.

I can't make up my mind whether I prefer to sandwich these cookies with Nutella, apricot jam, lemon curd, raspberry jam or raspberry jam AND buttercream. To solve this little problem, I often serve a selection of cookies sandwiched with different fillings and with different cut-out shapes. However you decide to serve them, they are buttery, nutty and quite lovely.

jammy dodgers

makes about 20

100 g/⅔ cup blanched hazelnuts, lightly toasted

225 g/15 tablespoons butter, soft

150 g/¾ cup (caster) sugar

1 teaspoon pure vanilla extract

2 large egg yolks

300 g/2¼ cups plain/all-purpose flour

½ teaspoon baking powder

5 tablespoons raspberry jam

5 tablespoons apricot jam or chocolate hazelnut spread

5 tablespoons lemon curd

icing/confectioners' sugar, for dusting

assorted cookie cutters, roughly 7 cm/2½ in. across

baking sheets, lined with parchment paper

small number, letter, heart and/or flower cookie cutters

Whizz the hazelnuts in a food processor until finely ground and set aside.

Cream the butter and sugar with an electric whisk or stand mixer until pale, light and fluffy – about 3 minutes in a stand mixer. Add the vanilla and egg yolks and mix until combined. Sift together the flour and baking powder, then gradually add to the creamed mixture, mixing after each addition. Add the ground hazelnuts and mix in. Lightly knead the dough until it comes together into a ball. Flatten into a disc, wrap in clingfilm/plastic wrap and refrigerate for 1 hour.

Light dust the work surface with flour and roll out the dough to a thickness of 2–3 mm/⅛ inch. Using the 7-cm/2½-inch cookie cutters, stamp out cookies and arrange on the prepared baking sheets. Gather the dough scraps together, press into a smooth-ish ball, re-roll and stamp out more cookies. Stamp out a small number, letter or shape from the middle of one half of the cookies. Refrigerate for 15 minutes.

Preheat the oven to 170°C (325°F) Gas 3.

Bake the cookies on the middle shelf of the oven for about 12–15 minutes or until golden. You might need to bake the cookies in batches. Allow the cookies to cool on the baking sheets for 5 minutes, then transfer to a wire rack and allow to cool completely.

Spread raspberry jam, apricot jam/chocolate hazelnut spread or lemon curd over the complete cookie halves. Dust icing/confectioners' sugar over the stamped-out number, letter, heart or flower halves and sandwich these on top of the jam layer.

These little ladybug cakes are a doddle to make and little hands will love helping out with the assembling. I have used white ready-to-roll royal icing/fondant/sugar paste as this is easier to find in most supermarkets but you could also use sugar paste that is pre-coloured – some larger supermarkets stock this in mixed packs and most sugarcraft suppliers will have a selection in a rainbow of colours. You will only need half the quantity of meringue buttercream from the recipe on page 12 but you can make up the full quantity and use the remainder to make Butterfly Cakes (page 90) to complete the insect theme.

ladybug cupcakes

makes 12

1 quantity Vanilla or Chocolate Cupcakes (page 8 or 9)

½ quantity Meringue Buttercream (page 12)

400 g/14 oz. ready-to-roll royal icing/fondant/sugar paste

red and black food colouring pastes

12-hole muffin pan, lined with paper cases

round cookie cutter, slightly wider than the widest part of the holes of the muffin pan

Preheat the oven to 180°C (350°F) Gas 4.

Prepare and bake the Vanilla or Chocolate Cupcakes as described on pages 8 or 9. Allow the cakes to rest in the pan for 3–4 minutes, then transfer to a wire rack and allow to cool completely.

Prepare the Meringue Buttercream as described on page 12. Spread a level tablespoon of buttercream smoothly over the top of each cupcake with a palette knife.

Break off a small nugget of ready-to-roll icing and wrap in clingfilm/plastic wrap until ready to use.

Take two-thirds of the remaining icing and tint it deep red by gradually adding the food colouring paste and kneading it in until fully incorporated. Tint the remaining one-third of the icing black and wrap in clingfilm/plastic wrap until ready to use. Be aware that both red and black food colouring pastes tend to get more intense after mixing and resting.

Lightly dust the work surface with icing/confectioners' sugar and roll out the red icing to a thickness of 2 mm/¹⁄₁₆ inch. Stamp out

12 discs using the cookie cutter. Lay a disc on top of each cake and gently smooth into place to completely cover the buttercream.

Lightly dust the work surface with icing/confectioners' sugar again and roll out the black icing to a thickness of no more than 2 mm/¹⁄₁₆ inch. Using the cookie cutter, stamp out 6 discs. Now stamp 2 leaf-shaped halves from each disc using the cutter. These are for the ladybug's head. Lightly brush a little cold water on the underside of each leaf shape and place on top of the red-covered cakes along one edge.

Using the blunt side of a knife, score a line down the middle of each ladybug from the middle of the head to the tail. Roll the off-cuts from the black icing into little balls and flatten into even-sized pairs of discs. Using a tiny dab of cold water, stick the discs in a symmetrical pattern on either side of each ladybug's back.

Make 24 small balls out of the reserved white icing and flatten slightly into discs. Stick 2 on each ladybug's head for eyes. Finally, finish the eyes with another small ball of black icing. Allow to set for an hour or so before serving.

I love these mini morsels –they are one delicious mouthful of light chocolatey cake, topped with a swirl of light-as-air marshmallow frosting and then coated in a crisp chocolate shell. The colourful sprinkles on top only add to the joy.

mini hi-hat cupcakes

makes 24

2 tablespoons unsweetened cocoa powder

3 tablespoons boiling water

75 g/5 tablespoons butter, soft

90 g/scant ½ cup (caster) sugar

1 large egg, beaten

1 teaspoon pure vanilla extract

75 g/⅔ cup plain/all-purpose flour

1 teaspoon baking powder

¼ teaspoon bicarbonate of/baking soda

a pinch of salt

1 tablespoon sour cream or milk

marshmallow topping

100 g/½ cup (caster) sugar

2 egg whites

tiny pinch of salt

to decorate

100 g/3½ oz. dark/bittersweet chocolate (60% cocoa solids)

50 g/1¾ oz. milk chocolate

½ teaspoon sunflower oil

assorted sugar sprinkles

2 x 12-hole mini muffin pans, lined with mini muffin cases

sugar thermometer

piping bag, fitted with a plain 1-cm/⅜-in. nozzle/tip

Preheat the oven to 180°C (350°F) Gas 4.

Tip the cocoa into a small bowl, add the boiling water and whisk until smooth. Set aside to cool slightly.

Cream the butter and sugar with an electric whisk or stand mixer until really pale, light and fluffy – at least 3 minutes. Gradually add the beaten egg, mixing well and scraping down the sides of the bowl between each addition. Add the vanilla and cocoa mixture and mix again until thoroughly combined.

Sift the flour, baking powder, bicarbonate of/baking soda and salt into the bowl, add the sour cream or milk and fold in using a rubber spatula or large metal spoon until smooth. Divide the mixture evenly between the paper cases and bake on the middle shelf of the preheated oven for about 15 minutes or until well risen and a skewer inserted into the middle of the cakes comes out clean.

Allow the cakes to rest in the pan for 3–4 minutes, then transfer to a wire rack and allow to cool completely.

To make the marshmallow topping, put the sugar, egg whites and salt in a heatproof bowl over a pan of simmering water. Whisk slowly until the sugar has dissolved and the mixture is foamy.

Continue cooking until the mixture reaches at least 60°C (140°F) on a sugar thermometer. Immediately pour the frosting into the bowl of a stand mixer fitted with the whisk attachment (or use an electric whisk and mixing bowl) and beat on medium speed until it will stand in stiff, glossy peaks – this will take about 3 minutes. Working quickly, scoop the frosting into the prepared piping bag. Pipe a swirl or coil on top of each cake and allow to set for about 30 minutes.

To decorate, melt both chocolates together with the oil in a heatproof bowl set over a pan of barely simmering water. Do not let the base of the bowl touch the water. Alternatively, melt them in a microwave on a low setting in short bursts. Remove from the heat and stir until smooth. Scoop into a small, deep bowl or tea cup and allow to cool slightly. Using a small, deep bowl or tea cup will make dipping the top of the cakes easier and ensure that the marshmallow is evenly coated.

Dip the marshmallow part of the cakes into the melted chocolate, allowing any excess to drip back into the bowl or cup. Allow to set for a couple of minutes, then scatter sugar sprinkles over the top and allow to set completely before serving.

These cakes bring a smile to my face every time I make them. Each adorable icing 'rubber duck' has its own slightly quizzical expression as it bobs along on a sea of buttercream and bubbles. Make the ducks in advance and allow them to dry for at least 24 hours. You could also make them from marzipan.

rubber ducky cupcakes

makes 12

200 g/6½ oz. ready-to-roll royal icing/fondant/sugar paste

orange, yellow, black and blue food colouring pastes

1 quantity Vanilla Cupcakes (page 8)

1 quantity Meringue Buttercream (page 12)

blue and white sugar pearls

baking sheet, lined with parchment paper

12-hole muffin pan, lined with paper cases

large piping bag, fitted with a large star-shaped nozzle/tip

The day before you want to bake the cake, make the rubber duckies.

Tint about 25 g/2 tablespoons of the ready-to-roll icing orange by gradually adding the food colouring paste and kneading it in until fully incorporated. Tint the remaining icing yellow in the same way. Cover the orange icing in clingfilm/plastic wrap until ready to use.

Start by making the ducks' bodies. Divide the yellow icing in half and wrap one half in clingfilm/plastic wrap. Divide the other half into 12 pieces and roll into balls in your hands. Pinch one side of each ball into a small peak for the duck's tail, place on the prepared baking sheet.

Take the remaining half of yellow icing, divide in half again, then divide one portion into 12 equal pieces. Roll each piece into a ball, then gently press onto each duck's body at the opposite side to the tail – this is the head. Divide the remaining yellow icing into 24 pieces and press into small wing shapes. Press one wing on each side of each duck.

To make the beaks, divide the orange icing into 12 pieces and shape into

3-dimensional triangles. Press one triangle onto the front of each duck head and gently form into a beak shape. Allow to dry for 2 hours.

After 2 hours, paint eyes onto each duck with a skewer dipped into the black food colouring paste.

The next day, preheat the oven to 180°C (350°F) Gas 4.

Prepare and bake the Vanilla Cupcakes as described on page 8. Allow the cakes to rest in the pan for 3–4 minutes, then transfer to a wire rack and allow to cool completely.

Prepare the Meringue Buttercream as described on page 12. Tint the buttercream pale blue using the food colouring paste. Spoon it into the prepared piping bag and pipe generous swirls on top of each cupcake.

Scatter the blue and white sugar pearls over the buttercream, then sit a rubber ducky on top just before serving.

Here's a neat and simple idea – cookies on a stick! Make a cookie
landscape for your party table or buy a block of foam from a florist,
cover it in foil or colourful tissue paper and push the lollies into it.

cookie pops

makes about 16

1 quantity Vanilla Shortbread
dough (page 10)

400 g/2⅔ cups royal icing sugar/
mix (or 2½ cups confectioners'
sugar mixed with 2 tablespoons
meringue powder)

assorted food colouring pastes

*cookie cutters in the shapes of
caterpillars, butterflies, ducks etc.*

*baking sheets, lined with
parchment paper*

about 16 oven-proof lollipop sticks

disposable piping bags

Prepare the Vanilla Shortbread dough as described on page 10. Flatten the dough
into a fat disc, wrap in clingfilm/plastic wrap and refrigerate until firm or for at
least 2 hours.

Lightly flour the work surface and roll the dough out to a thickness of about 3 mm/
⅛ inch. Using the cookie cutters, stamp out shapes from the dough and arrange
on the prepared baking sheets, allowing plenty of space between each one. Gather
the dough scraps together, press into a smooth-ish ball, re-roll and stamp out more
cookies. Push a lollipop stick into the bottom of each cookie so that it is completely
covered in dough and sticks into the cookie by about 2 cm/¾ inch. Refrigerate the
cookies for 20 minutes while you preheat the oven to 170°C (325°F) Gas 3.

Bake the cookies on the middle shelf of the preheated oven for about 12 minutes
or until pale golden – you may need to swap the sheets around halfway through
baking to ensure that the cookies brown evenly. Remove from the oven and allow
to cool on the baking sheets.

To make royal icing, tip the royal icing sugar/mix into a mixing bowl and whisk in
enough cold water to make a smooth icing that will just hold a ribbon trail when
the whisk is lifted from the bowl. Depending on the colour scheme and creatures
you have chosen, and the number of cookie shapes you are using, you will need
to divide the icing between smaller bowls and tint accordingly using food
colouring pastes.

Follow the instructions on page 11 to ice the cookies using the 'flooding' technique.
Allow to dry for at least 3 hours, and preferably overnight, before serving.

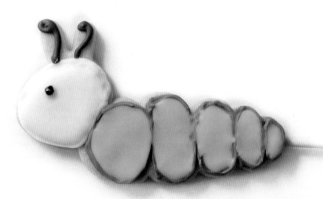

I love gingerbread houses in all shapes and sizes but I think this is my absolute favourite for its charm and quirkiness. You can go as wild as you like with the decorations, using homemade or storebought, as you wish. I have used a combination of the two in this instance. As for the birds, here is where you can really go to town. I'm rather fond of these particular feathered friends (available from craft supply stores) but you could make gingerbread birds iced in a variety of colours and sprinkles. If your artistic skills allow, paint a floral scene on the walls of the house using food colouring pastes.

gingerbread birdhouse

2 x quantities Gingerbread dough (page 10)

to decorate

2 tablespoons strawberry or apricot jam

300 g/10 oz. ready-to-roll royal icing/fondant/sugar paste

assorted food colouring pastes

400 g/2⅔ cups royal icing sugar/ mix (or 2½ cups confectioners' sugar mixed with 2 tablespoons meringue powder)

edible mimosa balls

white Sugar-paste Daisies (page 13)

butterfly sugar sprinkles

candy-coated chocolate drops

parchment paper or tracing paper for making templates

2 or 3 large baking sheets, lined with parchment paper

small round cookie cutter to accommodate your decorative birds

heart-shaped sugarcraft cutter

disposable piping bags

small, decorative birds

Prepare the Gingerbread dough as described on page 10, one batch at a time. Flatten each batch into a disc, wrap in clingfilm/plastic wrap and refrigerate for 1–2 hours.

While the dough is resting, cut out the paper templates for making the birdhouse. Lay a sheet of parchment or tracing paper over the outlines on pages 122–3 and trace the shapes needed for the birdhouse walls and roof. Cut out the shapes and write onto each template which shape it corresponds to – this will save confusion later. You will need one paper template for each shape.

Divide each portion of gingerbread dough into 3 equal pieces, making 6 in total. Lightly flour the work surface and roll out one piece of dough at a time to a thickness of 3 mm/⅛ inch. Lay each paper template onto a piece of dough and, using a sharp knife, cut around the templates. You will need 2 roof sections, 2 side walls and 2 end walls. Arrange all the shapes on the prepared baking sheets. (*See picture 1, overleaf*)

Using the cookie cutter, stamp out one hole from each end wall. Refrigerate the dough on the baking sheets for 30 minutes while you preheat the oven to 170°C (325°F) Gas 3.

Bake the gingerbread in batches on the middle shelf of the preheated oven for about 10–12 minutes until firm and starting to brown at the edges. Remove from the oven. While the gingerbread is still warm, lay the templates on top of the corresponding shapes and, using a long knife, trim the edges to neaten them if they have spread slightly during baking. Allow the gingerbread to cool on the baking sheets until completely cold.

To decorate, warm the jam to make it runny, then pass it through a sieve/strainer to remove any lumps. *Now turn to page 104.*

gingerbread birdhouse decoration

Divide the royal icing/fondant/sugar paste into 3 equal pieces. Tint one piece red by gradually adding the food colouring paste and kneading it in until fully incorporated. Tint another piece pale blue and leave the last piece white. Lightly dust the work surface with icing/confectioners' sugar and roll out the red icing to a thickness of about 2 mm/$\frac{1}{16}$ inch. Lay the roof template on top of the icing and, using a long knife, cut out 2 roof shapes.

Lightly brush a little warm jam over the top of each gingerbread roof tile and gently lay the red icing on top, smoothing into place with your hands and trimming off any excess with scissors or a sharp knife. Repeat with the blue icing for the side walls and the white icing for the end walls. Use the cookie cutter to stamp out the holes in the end walls after you have positioned the icing. (2)

Roll out any white icing off-cuts again and use to stamp out hearts. Stick them onto the roof using a tiny drop of cold water. Allow to dry for a good couple of hours.

When you are ready to assemble the birdhouse, it helps to have everything ready and if possible, a spare pair of hands to hold or pass things as needed. Prepare the royal icing first. Tip the royal icing sugar/mix into a mixing bowl and whisk in 1 teaspoon cold water at a time to make a smooth icing that is very thick and will hold a stiff peak when the whisk is lifted from the bowl. Spoon the icing into a disposable piping bag and snip the tip off the bag with scissors so that you can pipe a 2-mm/$\frac{1}{16}$-inch ribbon. Pipe an outline around the round cut-out on each of the end walls and stick the mimosa balls to it. (3)

Taking one side wall, pipe a thick line of icing on the bottom (long) edge and another up one of the short sides and hold this in place, long side down and gingerbread side innermost, on one side of a serving plate. This is where the extra hands come in useful. Now take one of the end walls and pipe icing along the bottom (short) edge and one of the side edges. Position this at right angles to the first wall on the plate, with the gingerbread side innermost. Press the 2 walls together to seal at the corners and hold securely in place for 1–2 minutes until the icing starts to stick. I find it helpful to use glasses or bottles to hold the walls in place while the icing is drying. (4)

Repeat with the second side and end walls – all of the corners should match up and the walls should gently lean outwards. For extra security, pipe more icing on the inside of the wall joins and another neater line on the outside. Leave the glasses or bottles in place against each wall until completely secure – this will take at least 30 minutes and longer to be on the safe side.

When the walls are secure, you are ready to attach the roof. Pipe a thick line of icing along the sloping pitch roof line and along the top of the walls. Taking one roof at a time, hold it in place so that the top of the roof panel lines up with the top of the pitch. Hold this until secure or wedge a glass underneath the roof panel to hold in place while you repeat with the second roof section. Allow to dry for least 30 minutes.

Use the royal icing to stick Gum-paste Daisies along the bottom joins of the house, butterflies along the corners of the walls and chocolate drops along the top of the roof. Allow to dry for a couple of hours before arranging the decorative birds in their house.

I'm not a huge fan of cake pops when they are made with packaged cake mix and frosting. And I'm not a fan of wastage in the kitchen but I do appreciate that sometimes you have leftover cake, especially if you are making the First Birthday Cakes on page 80, for instance. So why not use it up creatively and make cake pops? Kids seem to go nuts for them! I'm not so good at making cake pops into tricksy shapes or coating them in candy melts – I prefer a simple round pop shape and a crisp coating of melted chocolate. And then of course it gives you plenty of scope for going completely overboard with sprinkles.

cake pops

makes 20

75 g/2½ oz. dark/semisweet chocolate, chopped

400 g/14 oz. vanilla or chocolate cake

125 g/4 oz. cream cheese

25 g/1½ tablespoons butter, soft

200 g/1⅓ cups icing/confectioners' sugar, sifted

to decorate

400 g/14 oz. milk, dark/semisweet or white chocolate, chopped

assorted sugar sprinkles

baking sheet, lined with parchment paper

20 lollipop sticks

Melt the 75 g/2½ oz. dark/semisweet chocolate in a heatproof bowl set over a pan of barely simmering water. Do not let the base of the bowl touch the water. Alternatively, melt it in a microwave on a low setting in short bursts. Remove from the heat, stir until smooth and allow to cool slightly.

Take the cake and crumble it between your fingers into a bowl until it resembles coarse breadcrumbs.

In a separate large bowl, beat the cream cheese until smooth, add the butter and beat again. Gradually add the sifted sugar, mixing until smooth and thoroughly incorporated. Add the cooled, melted chocolate and mix again until smooth and silky. Add the cake crumbs and mix again with either a wooden spoon or your hands until the mixture is thoroughly combined and fudge-like in texture. (If your cake is very moist, you may not need to add all of the cream-cheese mixture.) Divide the mixture into 20 and, using your hands, roll each piece into a ball and arrange on the prepared baking sheet. Cover with clingfilm/plastic wrap and refrigerate until firm – 30–60 minutes.

To decorate, melt the chocolate as above. Take a lollipop stick and dip one end into the melted chocolate so that it comes about 2 cm/¾ inch up the stick. Now push the chocolate-coated stick into one of cake balls so that it is halfway through the ball. Repeat with the remaining sticks and cake balls. Refrigerate again for 10 minutes or until firm.

If the melted chocolate has started to firm up, gently re-melt it. Taking one cake pop at a time, dip it into the melted chocolate to completely coat and gently tap the stick on the side of the bowl to allow any excess chocolate to drip back into the bowl. Scatter sprinkles over the cake pop to coat and stand in a jar (or stick it in a block of florists' foam) in a cool place to set before serving. Repeat with the remaining cake pops.

These look almost too pretty to eat! In the recipe, I have given instructions for making chocolate and vanilla pinwheel cookies, but as you can see, we also prepared red and white cookies for the photograph opposite. To make the red and white pinwheels, simply prepare two plain batches of the vanilla shortbread dough, adding red food colouring paste to one of the batches at the same time as the egg. Then follow the instructions for rolling and assembling as below. This recipe does make quite a few cookies but they are quite small and do look beautiful popped into favour bags.

pinwheel cookies

makes about 50 small cookies

1 quantity Vanilla Shortbread dough (page 10)

1 quantity Chocolate Shortbread dough (page 11)

2 tablespoons milk

sugar sprinkles

2 baking sheets, lined with parchment paper

Prepare the Vanilla Shortbread dough and the Chocolate Shortbread dough as described on pages 10 and 11. Flatten each dough into a fat disc, wrap in clingfilm/plastic wrap and refrigerate until firm or for at least 2 hours.

Bring both of the doughs out of the fridge 15 minutes before you plan to roll them out so that they soften slightly. Lightly flour the work surface. You will find it easier to roll out half of the dough at a time, so weigh each dough and divide in half. Roll out one half of the vanilla dough to a rectangle roughly 20 x 40 cm/ 8 x 16 inches and with a thickness of about 2 mm/$\frac{1}{16}$ inch and move carefully to one side. Roll out one half of the chocolate dough into a rectangle the same size. Lightly brush milk over the top of the chocolate dough and carefully lay the vanilla dough on top. Using a long, sharp knife, trim the edges into a neat rectangle and cut in half again to give two 20 x 20-cm/8 x 8-inch squares. Working on one square at a time, roll the dough into a tight, even spiral – the roll should be about 6 cm/2½ inches thick. Wrap tightly in clingfilm/plastic wrap and refrigerate for 1 hour or until firm. Repeat with the remaining dough square and then repeat again with the unrolled remaining dough.

Any off-cuts of dough can be roughly kneaded together and rolled out to make crazy marble cookies!

Preheat the oven to 170°C (325°F) Gas 3.

Unwrap the dough logs and brush milk lightly all over them. Tip the sprinkles onto a tray and roll the shortbread logs in the sprinkles to completely coat the outsides in an even layer. Using a sharp knife, cut the shortbread logs into discs about 3 mm/$\frac{1}{8}$ inch thick and arrange on the prepared baking sheets. Bake in the preheated oven for about 10–12 minutes or until firm and pale golden in colour.

Allow the cookies to rest on the baking sheets for a couple of minutes, then transfer to a wire rack and allow to cool completely.

You may find it easier to bake and chill these cakes a day in advance – crumbs are less likely to spoil the buttercream.

building blocks

makes 16

1 quantity Vanilla Cupcakes (page 8, but follow the method on this page)

½ quantity Meringue Buttercream (page 12)

500 g/1 lb. ready-to-roll royal icing/fondant/ sugar paste

yellow, pink and blue food colouring pastes

150 g/1 generous cup royal icing sugar/mix (or 1 cup confectioners' sugar mixed with 2 teaspoons meringue powder)

16-hole mini square baking pan, greased and lightly dusted with flour, or a 23-cm/9-in. square baking pan, greased and lined with greased parchment paper

letter-shaped sugarcraft cutters

disposable piping bag

Preheat the oven to 180°C (350°F) Gas 4.

Prepare the Vanilla Cupcake mixture as described on page 8 and spoon into the prepared baking pan, filling each hole (or the plain baking pan, if using) no more than half full. Bake on the middle shelf of the oven for about 25 minutes until golden brown, well risen and a skewer inserted into the middle of the cake(s) comes out clean. Allow to rest in the pan for 5–10 minutes, then carefully turn out onto a wire rack and allow to cool completely. (If you have used a plain pan, cut the cooled cake into 16 squares.) Refrigerate until ready to decorate.

Prepare the Meringue Buttercream as described on page 12. If the tops of the cakes are too domed, level them using a sharp, serrated knife. Spread buttercream in a thin, even layer over the top and sides of each cake square. **(1)**

Divide the ready-to-roll icing into 3 and tint each portion a different colour by gradually adding the food colouring paste and kneading it in until fully incorporated. Lightly dust the work surface with icing/confectioners' sugar and take one portion of tinted icing (keep the others wrapped in clingfilm/plastic wrap until ready to use). Roll out to a thickness of 2 mm/¹⁄₁₆ inch. Using a template or ruler, cut out 5 squares to fit the sides of each block of cake. Press one square onto each of the 4 sides and the top of each building block, pinch the edges to seal and trim off any excess icing with scissors, if necessary. **(2)**

Gather the icing off-cuts, re-roll and stamp out shapes with the letter cutters – 5 in assorted colours for each building block. Stick in place with a dab of cold water. **(3)**

Repeat this whole process with the remaining 2 colours of icing and remaining building blocks. Tip the royal icing sugar/mix into a mixing bowl and whisk in enough cold water to make a smooth icing that will just hold a ribbon trail when the whisk is lifted from the bowl. Spoon it into the disposable piping bag and snip the very tip off the bag with scissors. Pipe a fine line along all of the edges on the building blocks. Allow to dry completely.

magic number cookies

It seems that pretty baking and pretty bunting go hand
in hand – and here I've taken it a GIANT step further
and created edible bunting. I've used large number
cookies but there's no reason why you couldn't use
letters or in fact any shape that takes your fancy.
Just remember to make a hole wide enough to thread
ribbon through in the top of each unbaked cookie.
You don't need any special piping or decorating skills
to make these look special either, just a steady hand
and a smattering of imagination. Why not get the kids
involved, too?

makes about 20 depending on size

1 quantity Vanilla Shortbread dough
(page 10)

300 g/2 generous cups royal icing
sugar/mix (or 2 cups confectioners'
sugar mixed with 4 teaspoons meringue
powder)

assorted food colouring pastes

large, number-shaped cookie cutters

*baking sheets, lined with parchment
paper*

disposable piping bags

fine, pretty ribbons

Prepare the Vanilla Shortbread dough as described on page 10. Flatten the dough into a fat disc, wrap in clingfilm/plastic wrap and refrigerate until firm or for at least 2 hours.

Lightly flour the work surface and roll the dough out to a thickness of about 3 mm/⅛ inch. Using the cookie cutters, stamp out numbers from the dough and arrange on the prepared baking sheets. Gather the dough scraps together, press into a smooth-ish ball, re-roll and stamp out more cookies. Using a skewer, push a 2-mm/¹⁄₁₆-inch hole into the top of each number so that you will be able to push a ribbon through it. Refrigerate the cookies for 20 minutes while you preheat the oven to 170°C (325°F) Gas 3.

Bake the cookies in batches on the middle shelf of the preheated oven for about 12 minutes or until pale golden. Remove from the oven and, while still warm, push the skewer into each hole again just in case it has shrunk and closed up slightly during baking. Leave the cookies on the baking sheets until completely cold.

To make royal icing, tip the royal icing sugar/mix into a mixing bowl and whisk in enough cold water to make a smooth icing that will hold a ribbon trail when the whisk is lifted from the bowl. Decide on how many colours you want in your icing colour scheme and divide the icing between bowls accordingly. Tint them using food colouring pastes.

Spoon each colour of icing into disposable piping bags and snip the very tip off the bag with scissors. Pipe lines and dots all over each cookie in a wild and crazy variety of designs – the wilder the better! Allow to dry for at least 3 hours.

When dry, thread pretty ribbons through each cookie and attach them to thicker ribbon to make cookie bunting.

Sometimes you don't want to go overboard with sprinkles and decorations and don't have the time for elaborate, tricky piping, and that's where this cake comes in. It's easy to make, delicious, banana-y and with the merest hint of chocolate. I have chosen not to frost this cake at all but simply to dust it with a flourish of icing/confectioners' sugar. However, if you'd like, you could drizzle a simple chocolate glaze over the top in a crazy zigzag pattern.

banana cake

serves 10

200 g/13 tablespoons butter, soft, plus 1–2 tablespoons extra for greasing

1–2 tablespoons unsweetened cocoa powder

300 g/2⅓ cups plain/all-purpose flour

2 teaspoons baking powder

½ teaspoon bicarbonate of/baking soda

a pinch of salt

4 ripe, medium bananas

3 tablespoons milk or sour cream, at room temperature

1 teaspoon pure vanilla extract

125 g/⅔ cup packed light brown (soft) sugar

100 g/½ cup (caster) sugar

4 large eggs, beaten

40 g/1½ oz. dark/bittersweet chocolate, grated

icing/confectioners' sugar, for dusting

kugelhopf/ring pan with a capacity of 2.5 litres/quarts

Preheat the oven to 180°C (350°F) Gas 4.

Melt the extra 1–2 tablespoons butter and use to thoroughly coat the inside of the cake pan, making sure that you grease all the creases thoroughly. Dust the pan with cocoa and tip out any excess.

Sift together the flour, baking powder, bicarbonate of/baking soda and salt.

In another bowl, mash the bananas and stir in the milk or sour cream and vanilla.

Cream the butter and sugars until pale, light and fluffy – about 3 minutes in a stand mixer. Gradually add the beaten eggs, mixing well and scraping down the side of the bowl between each addition. Fold in the sifted dry ingredients, followed by the banana mixture. Add the chocolate and mix gently until smooth and thoroughly combined.

Spoon the mixture into the prepared cake pan, spread level and bake on the middle shelf of the preheated oven for about 30–40 minutes or until well risen and a skewer inserted into the middle of the cake comes out clean.

Allow the cake to rest in the pan for no more than 2 minutes, then carefully turn out onto a wire rack and allow to cool completely. Dust with icing/confectioners' sugar to serve.

I love making cakes and cookies into fun face shapes. No matter how hard I try to make them identical, each of these pirates always ends up with a different expression or devilish grin, which I think is part of their charm. These are slightly more fiddly than some cupcakes due to the small details involved but the end result is more than worth it.

pirate cupcakes

makes 12

1 quantity Vanilla Cupcakes (page 8)

½ quantity Meringue Buttercream (page 12)

400 g/14 oz. ready-to-roll royal icing/fondant/sugar paste

red, blue and black food colouring pastes

gold sugar pearls

round sugar sprinkles in assorted colours

12-hole muffin pan, lined with paper cases

round cookie cutter, slightly wider than the widest part of the holes of the muffin pan

Preheat the oven to 180°C (350°F) Gas 4.

Prepare and bake the Vanilla Cupcakes as described on page 8. Allow the cakes to rest in the pan for 3–4 minutes, then transfer to a wire rack and allow to cool completely.

Prepare the Meringue Buttercream as described on page 12. Spread a level tablespoon of buttercream smoothly over the top of each cupcake with a palette knife.

Divide the ready-to-roll icing in half. Tint one half a very pale skin colour using the tiniest pin-prick of red food colouring paste and kneading it in until fully incorporated. Cover with clingfilm/ plastic wrap and set aside. Break off a small nugget of the remaining icing, leave this white and wrap in clingfilm/plastic wrap until ready to use. Divide the remaining icing into 3 equal portions and tint one portion red, one blue and one black. Cover each piece in clingfilm/plastic wrap until ready to use.

Lightly dust the work surface with icing/ confectioners' sugar and roll out the skin-coloured icing to a thickness of no more than 2 mm/¹⁄₁₆ inch. Stamp out 12 discs using the cookie cutter. Lay a disc on top of each cake and gently smooth into place to completely cover the buttercream. Gather the off-cuts together and roll out 12 small balls for the pirates' noses.

Lightly dust the work surface with a little more icing/confectioners' sugar and roll the red icing out to a thickness of 2 mm/¹⁄₁₆ inch. Using the cookie cutter again, stamp out 6 crescent shapes for the pirates' bandanas. Lightly brush a little cold water on the underside of each crescent shape and place on top of the pirates' faces along one edge. Repeat with the blue icing to make 6 blue bandanas.

Thinly roll out the black icing and, using a small, sharp knife, cut out moustache and eye patch shapes and arrange on the faces in the correct position. Stick the noses onto the faces with a little cold water. Roll the reserved white icing into tiny balls to make one eye for each pirate. Paint dots onto each eye with a skewer dipped into the black food colouring paste. Using a small piping nozzle, cutter or teaspoon, lightly score a mouth shape onto each pirate in a jaunty grin.

To finish, stick contrasting sugar sprinkles onto the bandanas and give each pirate a gold sugar-pearl earring.

Who doesn't like cookies and ice cream? No one I know, that's for sure! If you or your guests don't like peanuts, replace the peanut butter with regular butter and the peanuts with whatever nuts you prefer – walnuts or pecans work well. Raisins make a good substitute for chocolate chips, if you really must.

chocolate chip cookie ice cream sandwiches

makes about 20

175 g/1½ sticks butter, soft and cubed

75 g/⅓ cup peanut butter

175 g/¾ cup plus 2 tablespoons packed light brown (soft) sugar

75 g/⅓ cup golden caster or unrefined cane sugar

1 egg and 1 egg yolk, beaten

1 teaspoon pure vanilla extract

225 g/1⅔ cups plain/all-purpose flour

1 teaspoon bicarbonate of/baking soda

½ teaspoon baking powder

a pinch of salt

75 g/½ cup salted roasted peanuts, roughly chopped

150 g/1 cup chocolate chips (milk or dark/semisweet)

good-quality vanilla and chocolate ice cream, slightly softened

baking sheets, lined with parchment paper

Put the butter, peanut butter and sugars into the bowl of a stand mixer and beat until light and creamy. Add the beaten egg to the creamed mixture in 3 batches, mixing well between each addition. Add the vanilla and mix again.

Sift the flour, bicarbonate of/baking soda, baking powder and salt into the bowl and mix to just combine. Add the peanuts and chocolate chips and mix again until thoroughly combined. Wrap the dough in clingfilm/plastic wrap and refrigerate for at least 2 hours.

Preheat the oven to 170°C (325°F) Gas 3.

Roll the dough into balls no bigger than a walnut and arrange on the baking sheets, spacing them well apart. Slightly flatten each ball of dough with your hand and bake in batches on the middle shelf of the preheated oven for about 11 minutes or until golden. Remove from the oven and allow to cool on the baking sheets for 3–4 minutes, then transfer to a wire rack and allow to cool completely.

To serve, lay half of the cookies on the work surface, flat side uppermost. Top with a scoop of ice cream and sandwich together with another cookie. Eat immediately!

I am totally in love with this cupcake-cookie combination and so is my godson, Albie. They tick all the boxes as far as most little boys are concerned: cake, cookies, icing, frosting and nothing pink!

sailboat cupcakes

makes 12

½ quantity Vanilla Shortbread dough (page 10)

300 g/2 generous cups royal icing sugar/mix (or 2 cups confectioners' sugar mixed with 4 teaspoons meringue powder)

blue and red food colouring pastes

1 quantity Vanilla Cupcakes (page 8)

1 quantity Meringue Buttercream (page 12)

sailboat-shaped cookie cutter

baking sheet, lined with parchment paper

12 oven-proof lollipop sticks

disposable piping bags

12-hole muffin pan, lined with blue paper cases

Prepare the Vanilla Shortbread dough as described on page 10. Flatten the dough into a fat disc, wrap in clingfilm/plastic wrap and refrigerate until firm or for at least 2 hours.

Lightly flour the work surface and roll the dough out to a thickness of about 2 mm/ 1/16 inch. Using the cookie cutter, stamp out at least 12 shapes from the dough (you'll want a couple of spare sailboats in case of breakages!) and arrange on the prepared baking sheets, allowing plenty of space between each one. Push a lollipop stick into the bottom of each cookie so that it is securely embedded. Refrigerate the cookies for 20 minutes while you preheat the oven to 170°C (325°F) Gas 3.

Bake the cookies on the middle shelf of the preheated oven for about 12 minutes or until pale golden – you may need to swap the sheets around halfway through baking to ensure that the cookies brown evenly. Remove from the oven and allow to cool on the baking sheets.

To make royal icing, tip the royal icing sugar/ mix into a mixing bowl and whisk in enough cold water to make a smooth icing that will hold a ribbon trail when the whisk is lifted from the bowl. Divide the icing between 3 small bowls and leave one bowl white. Tint the second bowl of icing pale blue and the third red using the food colouring pastes. Cover the red and blue bowls with clingfilm/plastic wrap until ready to use.

Spoon 2–3 tablespoons of white icing into a disposable piping bag and cover the rest with

clingfilm/plastic wrap. Snip the very tip off the bag with scissors and pipe a fine outline for the sails on each cookie, plus a line for the mast. (See page 11 for instructions on flooding.) Spoon 2 tablespoons of red icing into another bag and pipe an outline for the hull. Allow to dry for about 10 minutes.

Spoon the white or blue icing onto the sail sections of the cookies within the icing outline. Use a mini palette knife, back of a teaspoon or a small knife to spread the icing in a smooth layer up to the outline. Repeat this with the red icing in the hull. Allow to dry for at least 30 minutes. Add a touch more food colouring to the blue icing to make it a deeper shade, spoon into another piping bag and pipe details onto each sail. Give each boat a small red flag at the top of the mast. Allow to dry for at least 3 hours.

Preheat the oven to 180°C (350°F) Gas 4 again. Prepare and bake the Vanilla Cupcakes as described on page 8. Allow the cakes to rest in the pan for 3–4 minutes, then transfer to a wire rack and allow to cool completely.

Prepare the Meringue Buttercream as described on page 12. Divide the buttercream between 2 bowls and, using food colouring paste, tint one bowl pale blue. Using a spoon, lightly marble the 2 buttercreams together. Cover the top of each cupcake with buttercream and use the back of the spoon to make waves. Push a sailboat onto each cupcake to serve.

gingerbread birdhouse templates

To make the Gingerbread Birdhouse on pages 102–105, you will need these templates. Lay a sheet of parchment paper or tracing paper over each outline on these pages, trace the outline, then cut out with scissors. Write onto each template which shape it corresponds to.

ROOF

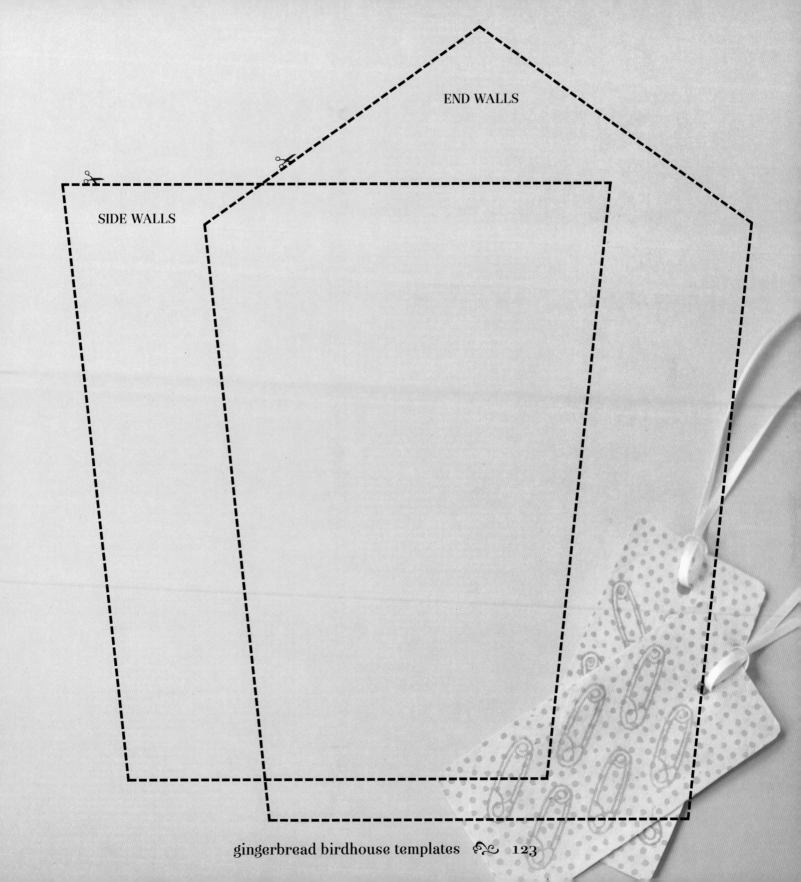

END WALLS

SIDE WALLS

stockists & suppliers

UK

Cakes Cookies & Crafts Shop

www.cakescookiesandcraftsshop.co.uk
Tel: 01524 389 684
Bakeware and cake decorations, plus an extensive range of Wilton piping bag nozzles/tips in all sorts of shapes and sizes. Also, sugar sprinkles, mimosa (sugar) balls, sugar pearls and lollipop sticks.

Jane Asher

www.jane-asher.co.uk
Tel: 020 7584 6177
Shop and online supplier of a wide range of cake baking and decorating supplies, for example tiny assorted cutters and embossing tools.

John Lewis

www.johnlewis.com
Tel: 08456 049 049
Lovely range of bakeware, from vintage-style mixing bowls and measuring cups to seasonal and shaped cupcake cases and pretty cookie cutters.

Lakeland

www.lakeland.co.uk
Tel: 01539 488 100
See online for details of your nearest store. Huge selection of kitchen and baking equipment, such as cupcake pans, cake decorations, storage containers, etc. Also, the mini-cake pan used in the Mini Fruitcakes on page 69 and Mini Victoria Sandwiches on page 74, as well as the special special square baking pan divided into 16 squares used in the Coffee & Hazelnut Cakes on page 54 and Building Blocks on page 111.

Shop Sweet Lulu

www.shopsweetlulu.com
Beautiful, cute and tasteful paraphernalia for parties, such as themed party/favour bags, boxes, straws, decorations, cupcake cases, twine and ribbon, gift tags, cake stands and balloons. US online store which will deliver internationally.

Sous Chef

www.souschef.co.uk
Tel: 0800 270 7591
Brilliant source of high-end, harder-to-find ingredients and items of kitchen equipment that usually has you trawling the internet for hours. The range isn't huge but there are very useful, small quantities of obscure and top-quality ingredients. Go here for disposable piping bags, freeze-dried raspberries and vanilla paste, for example.

Squires Kitchen

www.squires-shop.com
Tel: 0845 22 55 671
Large retailer of cake decorating and sugarcraft supplies with more than 4,000 products, eg. edible gold and silver leaf.

US

Bake It Pretty

www.bakeitpretty.com
Cute, vintage-inspired baking accoutrements.
eg. cupcake cases, sugarcraft cutters, lollipop sticks,
sugar pearls and sprinkles in every colour under the
sun, baby-themed cake toppers, pretty straws etc.

Crate & Barrel

www.crateandbarrel.com
Tel: 800 967 6696
Store and online supplier of kitchenware, such as
muffin pans, silicone bakeware, seasonal paper cases
and sugar/candy thermometers.

Global Sugar Art

www.globalsugarart.com
Tel: 800 420 6088
Cake-decorating supplies galore, eg. fondant, food
colouring pastes, lollipop sticks suitable for oven use,
and the special special square baking pan divided
into 16 squares used in the Coffee & Hazelnut Cakes
on page 54 and Building Blocks on page 111.

Kitchen Krafts

www.kitchenkrafts.com
Tel: 800 298 5389
Bakeware, candy, cake-decorating tools, icings,
cookie cutters and piping bags and nozzles/tips.

Michael's

www.michaels.com
Tel: 800 642 4235
Craft emporium with online store, plus stores all over
the US. It has an excellent selection of bakeware,
including fondant, gum paste, sugarcraft cutters,
ready-made gum-paste flowers and plenty more.

Shop Sweet Lulu

www.shopsweetlulu.com
See opposite.

Sugarcraft

www.sugarcraft.com
Every type of cake decoration imaginable,
plus boxes for presenting and carrying cupcakes,
cakes, and cookies as gifts.

Sur la Table

www.surlatable.com
Tel: 800 243 0852
Check online for details of your nearest store.
Offers bakeware including kugelhopf/bundt pans.
Good source for specialty ingredients too, such as
ready-to-roll royal icing. More than 70 retail stores
nationwide and an extensive online site.

Williams-Sonoma

www.williams-sonoma.com
Tel: 1 877 812 6235
Cupcake and muffin pans, cake stands, and more.

Wilton

www.wilton.com
The site to browse for all manner of baking and
decorating supplies. Packed with patterned and
themed paper cases, sprinkles, food colouring,
and decorations to suit every possible theme.

index

A

almonds
  chocolate and almond torte 77
  macarons 35
  praline 77
  rainbow cookies 44
  raspberry almond tartlets 28
    see also marzipan

B

baby battenburgs 19
baby bottle cookies 20
baby footprint cookies 39
banana cake 115
battenburgs, baby 19
birdhouse, gingerbread 102–5,
  122–3
birthday cakes 80–3
biscuits
  custard creams 32
  Viennese fingers 73
    see also cookies
bootees, sugar-paste/fondant 13
bottle cookies 20
brownie bites, double chocolate
  47
building blocks 111
buns, iced 66
buttercream 74
  meringue buttercream 12
butterfly cakes 90
buttermilk scones 70
button cookies 23

C

cake pops 107
cakes
  banana cake 115
  chocolate and almond torte 77
  daisy chain cake 57
  first birthday cakes 80–3
  gingerbread birdhouse 102–5,
    122–3
  malted milk chocolate cake
    with candle cookies 84–7
  pink and white layer cake 48
  spiced maple syrup cake 62
    see also cupcakes; small cakes
candle cookies 84–7
caramel, praline 77
cheesecake bites, New York 24

chocolate
  banana cake 115
  basic chocolate cupcakes 9
  cake pops 107
  chocolate and almond torte 77
  chocolate chip cookie ice
cream sandwiches 119
  chocolate shortbread 11
  double chocolate brownie bites
    47
  malted milk chocolate cake
    with candle cookies 84–7
  meringue buttercream 12
  mini hi-hat cupcakes 97
  pinwheel cookies 108
  rainbow cookies 44
  teddy bear cookies 40
  teddy bear cupcakes 89
  Viennese fingers 73
  white chocolate ganache 35
citrus coconut drizzle cakes 58
coconut
  citrus coconut drizzle cakes 58
coffee and hazelnut cakes 54
cookies
  baby bottle cookies 20
  baby footprint cookies 39
  basic gingerbread 10
  button cookies 23
  candle cookies 84–7
  chocolate chip cookie ice
    cream sandwiches 119
  cookie pops 101
  'flooding' 11
  gingerbread babies 43
  iced initial cookies 61
  jammy dodgers 93
  magic number cookies 112–13
  pinwheel cookies 108
  rainbow cookies 44
  sailboat cupcakes 120
  stroller cookies 31

  teddy bear cookies 40
    see also biscuits
cream
  lemon cream 35
  strawberry cream millefeuille
    51
  white chocolate ganache 35
cream cheese
  cake pops 107
  New York cheesecake bites 24
cupcakes
  basic chocolate cupcakes 9
  basic vanilla cupcakes 8
  ladybug cupcakes 94
  marbly swirl cupcakes 16
  mini hi-hat cupcakes 97
  pirate cupcakes 116
  pretty floral cupcakes 65
  rubber ducky cupcakes 98
  sailboat cupcakes 120
  teddy bear cupcakes 89
custard creams 32

D

daisy chain cake 57
decorations, sugar-paste/fondant
and gum-paste 13
double chocolate brownie bites
  47
dried fruit
  daisy chain cake 57
  mini fruitcakes 69
ducks
  rubber ducky cupcakes 98

F

first birthday cakes 80–3
'flooding' cookies 11
floral cupcakes 65
fondant shapes 13
footprint cookies 39
frangipane
  raspberry almond tartlets 28

frosting
  maple marshmallow frosting 62
  marshmallow frosting 12
fruitcakes
  daisy chain cake 57
  mini fruitcakes 69

G
ganache, white chocolate 35
ginger
  baby footprint cookies 39
  basic gingerbread 10
  gingerbread babies 43
  gingerbread birdhouse 102–5, 122–3
gum-paste shapes 13

H
hazelnuts
  coffee and hazelnut cakes 54
  jammy dodgers 93
hi-hat cupcakes 97

I
ice cream
  chocolate chip cookie ice cream sandwiches 119
iced buns 66
iced initial cookies 61
icing
  buttercream 74
  'flooding' cookies 11
  maple marshmallow frosting 62
  marshmallow frosting 12
  marshmallow topping 97
  meringue buttercream 12
  white chocolate ganache 35
initial cookies 61

J
jammy dodgers 93

L
ladybirds, sugar-paste/fondant 13
ladybug cupcakes 94
lemon
  citrus coconut drizzle cakes 58
  lemon cream 35
lime
  citrus coconut drizzle cakes 58

M
macarons 35
magic number cookies 112–13
malted milk chocolate cake with candle cookies 84–7
maple syrup
  spiced maple syrup cake 62
marbly swirl cupcakes 16
marshmallows 36
  maple marshmallow frosting 62
  marshmallow frosting 12
  marshmallow topping 97
marzipan
  baby battenburgs 19
  daisy chain cake 57
  mini fruitcakes 69
meringue buttercream 12
meringues 27
millefeuille, strawberry cream 51
mini fruitcakes 69
mini hi-hat cupcakes 97
mini Victoria sandwiches 74

N
New York cheesecake bites 24
numbers
  first birthday cakes 80–3
  magic number cookies 112–13
nuts
  daisy chain cake 57
  see also almonds, pistachios etc.

P
pastries
  strawberry cream millefeuille 51
peanut butter
  chocolate chip cookie ice cream sandwiches 119
pecans
  spiced maple syrup cake 62
pink and white layer cake 48
pinwheel cookies 108
pirate cupcakes 116
pistachios
  double chocolate brownie bites 47
pops
  cake pops 107
  cookie pops 101
praline 77
pretty floral cupcakes 65

R
rainbow cookies 44
raspberry almond tartlets 28
rattles, sugar-paste/fondant 13
rubber ducky cupcakes 98

S
sailboat cupcakes 120
scones, buttermilk 70
shortbread
  baby bottle cookies 20
  basic vanilla shortbread 10–11
  button cookies 23
  candle cookies 84–7
  chocolate shortbread 11
  cookie pops 101
  iced initial cookies 61
  magic number cookies 112–13
  pinwheel cookies 108
  sailboat cupcakes 120
  stroller cookies 31
  teddy bear cookies 40
small cakes

baby
battenburgs 19
  building blocks 111
  butterfly cakes 90
  citrus coconut drizzle cakes 58
  coffee and hazelnut cakes 54
  double chocolate brownie bites 47
  iced buns 66
  mini fruitcakes 69
  mini Victoria sandwiches 74
  rainbow cookies 44
  see also cupcakes
spiced maple syrup cake 62
sponge cakes
  basic chocolate cupcakes 9
  basic vanilla cupcakes 8
  first birthday cakes 80–3
strawberries
  pink and white layer cake 48
  strawberry cream millefeuille 51
stroller cookies 31
sugar-paste shapes 13

T
tartlets, raspberry almond 28
teddy bear cookies 40
teddy bear cupcakes 89
templates 122–3
torte, chocolate and almond 77

V
vanilla
  basic vanilla cupcakes 8
  basic vanilla shortbread 10–11
Victoria sandwiches, mini 74
Viennese fingers 73

acknowledgments

Once again the A-Team were brought back together for the making of this book. This is a team of very talented (and patient) ladies who don't bat an eyelid or think I've gone bonkers when I suggest making Gingerbread Birdhouses or Rubber Ducky Cupcakes.

So I owe a huge thank you to Kate for embracing this project and yet again creating beautiful pictures to illustrate my book. To Iona for her dedication, vision, gentle manner and wondrous talent in pulling the words and pictures into a cohesive and beautiful package. And to Jo for an endless supply of perfect tableware, ribbons and party pieces. And to Céline who right from the very start of a project, from concept, to planning, production and the final painstaking editing process, is nothing short of a joy to work with. I thank you.

And not forgetting Mike and Badger who put up with Mungo invading their home, having to be rescued from the neighbour's garden and deciding that your sofa was far more comfortable than his bed. He thanks you too.